Better Homes and Gardens®

ALL-TIME FAVORITE
Bread recipes

© 1979 by Meredith Corporation, Des Moines, Iowa.
All Rights Reserved. Printed in the United States of America.
First Edition. Third Printing, 1980.
Library of Congress Catalog Card Number: 78-74937
ISBN: 0-696-00185-3

On the cover: Favorite breads from your oven —clockwise from back left: tender *Molasses-Oatmeal Bread,* wholesome *Carrot Muffins,* and sweet *Apricot Daisy Ring.* (See Index for recipe pages.)

BETTER HOMES AND GARDENS® BOOKS

Editor-in-Chief: James A. Autry
Editorial Director: Neil Kuehnl
Executive Art Director: William J. Yates

Editor: Gerald M. Knox
Art Director: Ernest Shelton
Associate Art Directors: Randall Yontz,
    Neoma Alt West
Copy and Production Editors: David Kirchner,
    Lamont Olson, David A. Walsh
Assistant Art Director: Harijs Priekulis
Senior Graphic Designer: Faith Berven
Graphic Designers: Linda Ford, Richard Lewis,
    Sheryl Veenschoten, Tom Wegner

Food Editor: Doris Eby
Senior Associate Food Editor: Sharyl Heiken
Senior Food Editors: Sandra Granseth,
    Elizabeth Woolever
Associate Food Editors: Mary Cunningham,
    Diane Nelson, Joy Taylor, Pat Teberg
Recipe Development Editor: Marion Viall
Test Kitchen Director: Sharon Golbert
Test Kitchen Home Economists: Jean Brekke,
    Kay Cargill, Marilyn Cornelius, Maryellyn Krantz,
    Marge Steenson

All-Time Favorite Bread Recipes

Editors: Pat Teberg, Diane Nelson
Copy and Production Editor: David Kirchner
Graphic Designer: Tom Wegner

Our seal assures you that every recipe in *All-Time Favorite Bread Recipes* is endorsed by the Better Homes and Gardens Test Kitchen. Each recipe is tested for family appeal, practicality, and deliciousness.

Contents

FAVORITE HOME-BAKED BREADS

If you're the type who savors the aroma of warm-from-the-oven yeast breads, enticing coffee cakes, or hot muffins generously buttered, you'll enjoy this book.

Our collection of *All-Time Favorite Bread Recipes* will make you a master at the art of bread baking, whether it be yeast breads or quick breads.

If you're a newcomer to bread baking, you'll find easy-to-follow directions and step-by-step illustrations to guarantee perfect results.

And for those of you who've already mastered the basics, expand your repertoire to include decoratively shaped coffee cakes, dinner rolls, and sweet rolls. Then help yourself to the unique flavor of sourdough in our special section of sourdough recipes.

Yeast Bread Tips
When making yeast breads, you'll want your loaves to look and taste extra special. Below are some helpful hints we recommend for achieving a perfect product every time.
• Although you can still make bread the conventional "soften-the-yeast" way, consider the newer easy-mix method. It eliminates the yeast-softening step since you combine the dry yeast directly with the flour.
• Here's how to identify the stage of dough specified for your bread: *Soft dough* is too sticky to knead and is often used for batter breads. *Moderately soft dough* is slightly sticky, kneads easily on a floured surface, and is used for most sweet breads. *Moderately stiff dough* is somewhat firm to the touch, kneads easily on a floured surface, and is used for most unsweet breads. *Stiff dough* is firm to the touch and is easily rolled on a floured surface. French bread dough is stiff.

• When the recipe gives a range on the amount of flour, start by adding the smaller amount. And remember, flour used in kneading is also part of this measured amount.
• Do not add flour after rising starts. This causes dark streaks and a coarse texture.
• On humid days, the dough may require more flour than stated in the recipe.
• Tap the crust with your finger to test for doneness. A hollow sound indicates that the bread is done.
• Immediately removing the baked bread from the pan keeps it from steaming. Place the loaf on a wire rack to cool.
• To achieve various crusts, gently brush the top before baking. Use shortening, butter, margarine, or oil for a browner crust. Brush with milk, water, or beaten egg for a crispy and shiny crust. For a softer crust, brush the top with butter or margarine after baking.

Flours and Grains

All-Purpose Flour is a blend of hard and soft wheat that produces a constantly dependable flour. It gives the best results with a wide variety of baked goods.

Self-Rising Flour is an all-purpose flour to which baking powder and salt have been added. One cup of self-rising flour contains 1½ teaspoons of baking powder and ½ teaspoon of salt.

Whole Wheat Flour (or graham flour) contains the entire wheat kernel — bran, germ, and endosperm (nutritive plant tissue). In all-purpose flour, only the endosperm is used.

Rye Flour is available in light, medium, or dark versions. It is second to whole wheat flour in the amount of gluten protein (needed for yeast-bread structure) it contains.

Rice Flour may be milled from brown or white rice. It is used most frequently for gluten-restricted diets.

Wheat Germ is the germinating portion of the wheat kernel.

Cornmeal (ground corn) and *Rolled Oats* (oat groats pressed between rollers) give a crunchy sweetness to breads.

High-Altitude Baking

Almost every ingredient in breads is affected by the lower air pressure at high altitudes, especially leavenings, liquids, and sugar.

Leavenings: With less air pressure to control expansion, baked products rise too quickly and textures are coarse and crumbly.

Liquids: Evaporation is accelerated at high elevations, causing breads to dry.

Sugar: As liquid evaporates, sugar becomes more concentrated. This weakens the cell structure of breads, causing them to fall.

Quick-bread batters are fairly stable and need little adjustment, but it is recommended that you experiment, reducing the sugar and baking powder and increasing the liquid.

Yeast bread doughs rise more quickly at high altitudes, resulting in a weaker structure. To compensate, shorten the rising time. You may need to add extra liquid to compensate for rapid evaporation during rising.

Making Sour Milk

When you don't have any buttermilk on hand, substitute an equal amount of "soured" milk for the buttermilk.

To make sour milk, combine 1 tablespoon *lemon juice or vinegar* and enough whole *milk* to make *1 cup* total liquid. Let mixture stand 5 minutes before using in the recipe.

Easy-Mix Method

Do not use the easy-mix method in Canada. Differences in the yeast make it impossible to get good results. Instead, here's how to convert recipes to the conventional method. Change ¼ *cup* of the liquid to warm *water;* add yeast to dissolve. Heat remaining liquid and continue as directed in the conventional method (see page 10).

1 YEAST BREADS

This selection of homemade yeast breads includes (clockwise from back left) *Yeast Doughnuts*, apricot-filled *Lattice Coffee Cake*, *Glazed Orange Rolls*, buttery *Croissants*, filled *Pita Bread*, sesame-topped *Soft Pretzels*, and pimiento-flecked *Cheese Braid*. (See Index for recipe pages.)

Loaves

Easy-Mix White Bread

5¾ to 6¼ cups all-purpose flour
1 package active dry yeast
2¼ cups milk
2 tablespoons sugar
1 tablespoon shortening
2 teaspoons salt

In large mixer bowl combine 2½ cups of the flour and the yeast. In saucepan heat milk, sugar, shortening, and salt just till warm (115° to 120°) and shortening is almost melted; stir constantly. Add to flour mixture (step 1). Beat at low speed of electric mixer ½ minute, scraping sides of bowl. Beat 3 minutes at high speed (step 2). Stir in as much of the remaining flour as you can mix in with a spoon (step 3). Turn out onto lightly floured surface. Knead in enough remaining flour to make a moderately stiff dough that is smooth and elastic, 6 to 8 minutes total (steps 4-5). Shape into a ball (step 6). Place in lightly greased bowl; turn once to grease surface. Cover; let rise in warm place till double, about 1¼ hours (step 7).

Punch down; turn out onto lightly floured surface (step 8). Divide dough in half. Cover; let rest 10 minutes. Lightly grease two 8x4x2-inch loaf pans. Shape each half of dough into a loaf by patting or rolling. To pat dough, gently pull the dough into a loaf shape, tucking the edges beneath. To roll, refer to step 9. Brush loaves with melted butter. Cover; let rise in warm place till nearly double (45 to 60 minutes). Bake in 375° oven about 45 minutes or till done. Test by tapping the top with your finger. A hollow sound means the loaf is properly baked. If top browns too fast, cover loosely with foil the last 15 minutes of baking. Remove from pans; cool. Makes 2 loaves.

1

Pour heated milk mixture over flour mixture in mixer bowl. Since the yeast is mixed with the flour, the temperature of the milk mixture can be higher (115° to 120°) than the water used to dissolve yeast in the conventional method (110° to 115°); see page 10.

2

Beat mixture at low speed of electric mixer for ½ minute, scraping sides of bowl constantly. Beat mixture at high speed for 3 minutes. Batter should be smooth and well blended, as shown.

3

Stir in as much of the remaining 3¾ cups flour as you can mix in with a spoon. It's helpful to measure out the remaining 3¾ cups flour before starting to add it to the dough. This way, you won't lose count if you're interrupted while measuring. Do not try to use your electric mixer for this step unless it is specially equipped to handle heavy doughs.

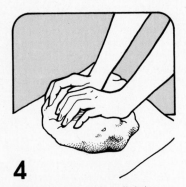

4

Turn dough out onto lightly floured surface. Using a well-floured pastry cloth makes the dough easy to knead using the minimum amount of flour.

Knead in enough of the remaining flour to make a moderately stiff dough that is smooth and elastic. To knead, fold the dough over and push down with the heels of your hands, curving your fingers over the dough, as shown.

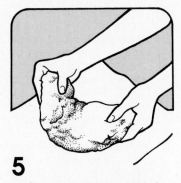

5

Give the dough a quarter turn, then fold over and push down again. Kneading is important in determining the final structure of the loaf, as it develops the gluten of the flour. If the dough is not kneaded enough, the loaf will be more likely to have a coarse texture, and will probably not rise as high in the pan.

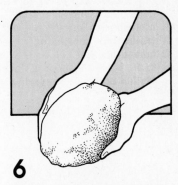

6

Continue kneading in the fold-push-turn procedure till dough is smooth and elastic, as shown. Shape into a ball.

To be sure you've kneaded enough, set a timer for the time suggested in the recipe. You may want to stop and rest a bit instead of kneading the dough all at once. Just be sure the total time is as long as the recipe suggests.

7

Dough should be allowed to rise until it doubles in size. Times suggested in the recipes are guidelines. The actual time needed may be a little more or less than that indicated. The dough is ready to shape when you can lightly and quickly press two fingertips ½ inch into the dough and the indentation remains, as shown.

8

Punch down the dough by pushing your fist into the center of the dough, as shown. Then pull the edges of the dough to the center, turn dough over, and place on a lightly floured surface.

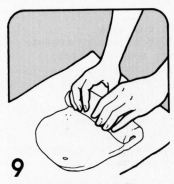

9

To shape dough by rolling, place ball of dough on a lightly floured pastry cloth or board. Roll into a 12x8-inch rectangle, rolling to the outer edges to remove all the bubbles. Roll up tightly, starting with narrow edge. Seal with fingertips as you roll. Repeat to make second loaf.

White Bread (conventional method)

1 **package active dry yeast**
¼ **cup warm water (110° to 115°)**
2 **cups milk**
2 **tablespoons sugar**
1 **tablespoon shortening**
2 **teaspoons salt**
5¾ **to 6¼ cups all-purpose flour**
   Melted butter *or* margarine

Soften yeast in warm water. In saucepan heat milk, sugar, shortening, and salt just till warm (115° to 120°) and shortening is almost melted; stir constantly. Turn into large mixing bowl. Stir in *2 cups* of the flour; beat well. Add the softened yeast; stir till smooth. Stir in as much of the remaining flour as you can mix in with a spoon. Turn out onto lightly floured surface. Knead in enough of the remaining flour to make a moderately stiff dough that is smooth and elastic (6 to 8 minutes total). Shape into a ball. Place in lightly greased bowl; turn once to grease surface. Cover; let rise in warm place till double (about 1¼ hours).

Punch down; turn out onto lightly floured surface. Divide dough in half. Shape into two balls. Cover; let rest 10 minutes. Grease two 8x4x2-inch loaf pans. Shape each ball of dough into a loaf (see pages 8-9). Place in pans. Brush loaves with some melted butter or margarine. Cover; let rise in warm place till nearly double (45 to 60 minutes). Bake in 375° oven about 45 minutes or till bread tests done. Remove from pans; cool on wire rack. Makes 2 loaves.

Note: To make bread ahead, prepare dough for White Bread, using either the conventional or easy-mix method (see page 8). Cover loaves loosely with clear plastic wrap. Refrigerate up to 24 hours. When ready to bake, remove bread from refrigerator and uncover. Brush with some melted butter or margarine. Let stand in warm place till loaves nearly double; puncture any surface bubbles with a wooden pick. Bake as above.

Crusty Onion Bread

2¼ **cups water**
½ **of a 1¼-ounce envelope onion**
   soup mix (¼ cup)
2 **tablespoons shortening**
1 **tablespoon sugar**
1 **teaspoon salt**
5½ **to 6 cups all-purpose flour**
1 **package active dry yeast**
   Cornmeal
1 **slightly beaten egg white**
1 **tablespoon water**

In saucepan combine the 2¼ cups water and dry soup mix; cover and simmer 10 minutes. Stir in shortening, sugar, and salt; cool mixture to 115° to 120°. In large mixer bowl combine *2½ cups* of the flour and yeast; add onion mixture. Beat at low speed of electric mixer for ½ minute, scraping sides of bowl constantly. Beat at high speed for 3 minutes. Stir in as much of the remaining flour as you can mix in with a spoon. Turn out onto lightly floured surface. Knead in enough of the remaining flour to make a moderately stiff dough that is smooth and elastic (6 to 8 minutes total). Shape into a ball. Place in lightly greased bowl; turn once. Cover; let rise in warm place till double (about 1 hour).

Punch down. Turn out onto lightly floured surface; divide in half. Cover; let rest 10 minutes. Shape into two 12-inch loaves. Place each on greased baking sheet sprinkled with cornmeal. Cover; let rise till nearly double (about 30 minutes). With sharp knife, make diagonal cuts 2½ inches apart and ¼ inch deep across tops of loaves.

Bake in 375° oven 20 minutes. Brush loaves with mixture of beaten egg white and 1 tablespoon water. Bake 10 minutes more. Remove from baking sheets; cool thoroughly on wire rack. Makes 2 loaves.

French Bread

5½ to 6 cups all-purpose flour
2 packages active dry yeast
2 teaspoons salt
2 cups warm water (115° to 120°)
 Cornmeal
1 slightly beaten egg white
 (optional)
1 tablespoon water (optional)

In large mixer bowl combine *2 cups* of the flour, the yeast, and salt. Add warm water. Beat at low speed of electric mixer for ½ minute, scraping sides of bowl constantly. Beat 3 minutes at high speed. Stir in as much of the remaining flour as you can mix in with a spoon. Turn out onto lightly floured surface. Knead in enough of the remaining flour to make a stiff dough that is smooth and elastic (8 to 10 minutes total). Shape into a ball. Place in lightly greased bowl; turn once to grease surface. Cover; let rise in warm place till double (1 to 1¼ hours).

Punch down; turn out onto lightly floured surface. Divide in half. Cover; let rest 10 minutes. Roll each half into a 15x12-inch rectangle. Roll up tightly from long side; seal well. Taper ends. (Or, shape into individual loaves or hard rolls as below.) Place, seam side down, on greased baking sheet sprinkled with cornmeal. If desired, brush with mixture of egg white and water. Cover; let rise till nearly double (about 45 minutes). With sharp knife, make 3 or 4 diagonal cuts about ¼ inch deep across tops of loaves. Bake in 375° oven 40 to 45 minutes. If desired, brush again with egg-white mixture after 20 minutes of baking. Cool. Makes 2 loaves.

Individual loaves: Cut each half of dough into quarters, making 8 pieces total. Shape into balls. Cover; let rest 10 minutes. Shape each ball into a 6-inch loaf; taper ends. Place 2½ inches apart on greased baking sheet sprinkled with cornmeal. Press down ends of loaves. Brush with egg-white mixture, if desired. Cover; let rise till nearly double (about 45 minutes). Make 3 shallow cuts diagonally across top of each. Bake in 375° oven for 25 to 30 minutes. If desired, brush again with egg-white mixture after 15 minutes of baking. Makes 8 loaves.

Hard rolls: Cut each half of dough into eighths, making 16 pieces total. Shape into rolls; place 2 inches apart on greased baking sheet sprinkled with cornmeal. Brush with egg-white mixture, if desired. Cover; let rise till nearly double (about 45 minutes). Cut a shallow crisscross in tops. Bake in 375° oven 25 to 30 minutes. If desired, brush again with egg-white mixture after baking 15 minutes. Makes 16.

Note: Italian Bread is similar to French Bread, but loaves are often shorter and thicker.

Quick-Rye Bread

1 13¾-ounce package hot roll mix
¾ cup warm milk (110° to 115°)
1 egg
¼ cup molasses
¾ cup rye flour
2 teaspoons caraway seed
½ teaspoon salt

Remove yeast packet from hot roll mix package. In large mixing bowl dissolve yeast in warm milk. Stir in the egg and molasses. Stir together the flour from the hot roll mix and the rye flour. Stir in caraway seed and salt. Add to yeast mixture; mix well.

Turn dough out onto lightly floured surface. Knead till smooth and elastic (12 to 15 strokes). Shape into two balls. Place each on greased baking sheet; flatten to a 5-inch diameter. Cover; let rise in warm place till nearly double (about 1 hour). Bake in 350° oven about 25 minutes or till done. Cool. Makes 2 loaves.

Egg Bread

6¾ to 7¼ cups all-purpose flour
2 packages active dry yeast
2 cups milk
¼ cup sugar
¼ cup butter *or* margarine
2 teaspoons salt
3 eggs

In large mixer bowl combine *3 cups* of the flour and the yeast. In saucepan heat milk, sugar, butter, and salt just till warm (115° to 120°) and butter is almost melted; stir constantly. Add to flour mixture; add eggs. Beat at low speed of electric mixer ½ minute, scraping bowl. Beat 3 minutes at high speed. Stir in as much remaining flour as you can mix in with a spoon. Turn out onto lightly floured surface. Knead in enough remaining flour to make a moderately stiff dough that is smooth and elastic (6 to 8 minutes total). Shape into a ball. Place in lightly greased bowl; turn once to grease surface. Cover; let rise in warm place till double (about 1¼ hours).

Punch down; divide dough in half. Cover; let rest 10 minutes. Shape into two loaves. Place in two greased 9x5x3-inch loaf pans. Cover; let rise till nearly double (35 to 45 minutes). Bake in 375° oven for 35 to 40 minutes or till done, covering with foil the last 15 minutes to prevent overbrowning. Remove from pans; cool on wire rack. Makes 2 loaves.

Cinnamon Swirl Bread: Prepare Egg Bread dough. Instead of shaping into loaves, roll each half of dough into a 15x7-inch rectangle. Brush entire surface lightly with water. Combine ½ cup *sugar* and 2 teaspoons ground *cinnamon*; sprinkle *half* the sugar mixture over each rectangle. Beginning with narrow end, roll up jelly-roll-style; seal edge and ends. Place, sealed edges down, in greased loaf pans. Continue as directed above. Drizzle warm loaf with Confectioners' Icing (see recipe, page 34), if desired.

Raisin Bread: Prepare Egg Bread dough as directed, *except* stir in 2 cups plumped *raisins* when stirring in flour with a spoon. To plump raisins, cover raisins in saucepan with water. Bring to boiling. Remove from heat and let stand 5 minutes; drain. Drizzle warm loaf with Confectioners' Icing (see recipe, page 34), if desired.

Herbed Bread: Prepare Egg Bread dough as directed, *except* combine 2 tablespoons *dried parsley flakes*; 1 tablespoon *dried tarragon,* crushed; and 1 teaspoon *celery seed* with 3 cups flour and the yeast.

Swedish Limpa

3¼ to 3¾ cups all-purpose flour
2 packages active dry yeast
1 tablespoon caraway seed
½ teaspoon fennel seed (optional)
2 cups warm water (115° to 120°)
½ cup packed brown sugar
2 tablespoons finely shredded
  orange peel
1 tablespoon cooking oil
1 teaspoon salt
2½ cups rye flour

In large mixer bowl combine 2½ cups of the all-purpose flour, the yeast, caraway seed, and fennel seed. Stir together water, brown sugar, orange peel, oil, and salt. Add to flour mixture. Beat at low speed of electric mixer for ½ minute, scraping bowl. Beat 3 minutes at high speed. Stir in rye flour and as much remaining all-purpose flour as you can mix in with a spoon. Turn out onto floured surface. Knead in enough remaining flour to make a moderately stiff dough that is smooth and elastic (6 to 8 minutes total). Place in greased bowl; turn once. Cover; let rise in warm place till double (1¼ to 1½ hours).

Punch down; divide in half. Cover; let rest 10 minutes. Shape into two 4½-inch round loaves on greased baking sheet. Cover; let rise till nearly double (about 40 minutes). Bake in 350° oven 40 to 45 minutes. Cool. Makes 2.

Slice into this attractive loaf of *Cinnamon Swirl Bread*. Drizzled with Confectioners'
Icing, this cinnamon- and sugar-filled bread is one of several delicious *Egg Bread* variations.

Sweet Banana Bread

5½ to 6 cups all-purpose flour
2 packages active dry yeast
¾ cup milk
½ cup sugar
½ cup butter *or* margarine
1 teaspoon salt
2 ripe bananas, mashed (1 cup)
2 eggs
1 teaspoon water

In bowl combine *2 cups* flour and the yeast. Heat milk, sugar, butter, and salt just till warm (115° to 120°); stir constantly. Add to flour mixture; add bananas, 1 egg, and 1 egg yolk (reserve egg white). Beat at low speed of electric mixer ½ minute, scraping bowl. Beat 3 minutes at high speed. Stir in as much remaining flour as you can mix in with a spoon. Turn out onto lightly floured surface. Knead in enough remaining flour to make a moderately stiff dough (6 to 8 minutes). Shape into a ball. Place in greased bowl; turn once. Cover; let rise till double (about 1 hour).

Punch down; divide in half. Cover; let rest 10 minutes. Shape into two round loaves; place on greased baking sheets. Flatten slightly with palm of hand to 6- to 7-inch diameter. Combine reserved egg white and water; brush tops. Cover; let rise till nearly double (30 to 45 minutes). Bake in 325° oven 35 to 40 minutes. Cool. Makes 2.

Pumpernickel

2¾ to 3¼ cups all-purpose flour
3 packages active dry yeast
1 tablespoon caraway seed
1½ cups warm water (115° to 120°)
½ cup light molasses
2 tablespoons cooking oil
1 tablespoon salt
2 cups rye flour
  Cornmeal

In large mixer bowl combine *2 cups* of the all-purpose flour, the yeast, and caraway. Mix water, molasses, oil, and salt. Add to flour mixture. Beat at low speed of electric mixer ½ minute, scraping bowl. Beat 3 minutes at high speed. Stir in rye flour and as much remaining all-purpose flour as you can mix in with a spoon. Turn out onto lightly floured surface. Knead in enough of the remaining all-purpose flour to make a moderately stiff dough that is smooth and elastic (6 to 8 minutes total). Shape into a ball. Place in lightly greased bowl; turn once. Cover; let rise in warm place till double (about 1½ hours).

Punch down; divide in half. Cover; let rest 10 minutes. Shape into two round loaves. Place on greased baking sheet sprinkled with cornmeal. Flatten slightly with hand to 6- to 7-inch diameter. Cover; let rise till nearly double (30 to 45 minutes). Bake in 350° oven 35 to 40 minutes or till well browned. Remove from baking sheet; cool. Makes 2.

Bran Bread

2½ to 3 cups all-purpose flour
1 package active dry yeast
1 cup milk
1 cup whole bran cereal
2 tablespoons honey
2 tablespoons butter *or* margarine
1 teaspoon salt
1 egg

In bowl combine *1 cup* flour and the yeast. Heat milk, bran, honey, butter, and salt just till warm (115° to 120°); stir constantly. Add to flour mixture; add egg. Beat at low speed of electric mixer ½ minute, scraping bowl. Beat 3 minutes at high speed. Stir in as much remaining flour as you can mix in with a spoon. Turn out onto lightly floured surface. Knead in enough remaining flour to make a moderately stiff dough (6 to 8 minutes). Shape into a ball. Place in lightly greased bowl; turn once. Cover; let rise in warm place till double (1 to 1¼ hours).

Punch down. Cover; let rest 10 minutes. Shape into loaf. Place in greased 8x4x2-inch loaf pan. Cover; let rise till nearly double (about 45 minutes). Bake in 375° oven about 30 minutes, covering with foil the last 15 minutes to prevent overbrowning. Remove from pan; cool. Makes 1 loaf.

Cheese Braid (pictured on pages 6 and 7)

4 to 4½ cups all-purpose flour
1 package active dry yeast
1½ cups milk
2 tablespoons sugar
1½ teaspoons salt
1 egg
2 cups shredded American
    cheese (8 ounces)
2 tablespoons chopped pimiento
    (optional)

In large mixer bowl combine *2 cups* flour and the yeast. Heat and stir milk, sugar, and salt just till warm (115° to 120°). Add to flour mixture; add egg and cheese. Beat at low speed of electric mixer ½ minute, scraping bowl. Beat 3 minutes at high speed. Stir in pimiento, if desired. Stir in as much remaining flour as you can mix in with a spoon. Turn out onto lightly floured surface. Knead in enough remaining flour to make a moderately stiff dough that is smooth and elastic (6 to 8 minutes total). Shape into a ball. Place in greased bowl; turn once. Cover; let rise in warm place till double (about 1½ hours).

Punch down; divide into 6 portions. Cover; let rest 10 minutes. Roll each portion into a rope 15 inches long. Shape into two braids using 3 ropes for each on greased baking sheets (refer to tip on page 45). Cover; let rise till nearly double (35 to 45 minutes). Bake in 375° oven 15 to 20 minutes. Cool. Makes 2 braids.

Whole Wheat Bread

4½ to 5 cups whole wheat flour
2 packages active dry yeast
1¾ cups milk
⅓ cup packed brown sugar
2 tablespoons shortening
2 teaspoons salt

In large mixer bowl combine *2 cups* flour and the yeast. Heat milk, brown sugar, shortening, and salt just till warm (115° to 120°) and shortening is almost melted; stir constantly. Add to flour mixture. Beat at low speed of electric mixer ½ minute, scraping bowl. Beat 3 minutes at high speed. Stir in as much remaining flour as you can mix in with a spoon. Turn out onto lightly floured surface. Knead in enough remaining flour to make a moderately stiff dough that is smooth and elastic (6 to 8 minutes total). Shape into a ball. Place in lightly greased bowl; turn once. Cover; let rise in warm place till double (1 to 1½ hours).

Punch down; turn out onto lightly floured surface. Cover; let rest 10 minutes. Shape into loaf; place in greased 9x5x3-inch loaf pan. Cover; let rise till nearly double (about 30 minutes). Bake in 375° oven 35 to 40 minutes. Cover with foil the last 20 minutes to prevent overbrowning. Remove from pan; cool on wire rack. Makes 1 loaf.

Anadama Bread

6¼ to 6¾ cups all-purpose flour
½ cup cornmeal
2 packages active dry yeast
2 cups water
½ cup dark molasses
⅓ cup shortening
1 tablespoon salt
2 eggs
    Melted shortening

In mixer bowl combine *3 cups* flour, cornmeal, and yeast. Heat water, molasses, shortening, and salt just till warm (115° to 120°); stir constantly. Add to flour mixture; stir in eggs. Beat at low speed of electric mixer ½ minute. Beat 3 minutes at high speed. Stir in as much remaining flour as you can mix in with a spoon. Turn out onto lightly floured surface. Knead in enough remaining flour to make a moderately soft dough that is smooth and elastic (3 to 5 minutes total). Shape into a ball in greased bowl; turn once. Cover; let rise in warm place till double (1 to 1¼ hours).

Punch down; divide in half. Cover; let rest 10 minutes. Grease two 9x5x3-inch loaf pans. Shape dough into 2 loaves; place in pans. Cover; let rise till double (45 to 60 minutes). Bake in 375° oven 35 to 40 minutes. Makes 2.

Potato Bread

1 **medium potato, peeled and cubed**
1½ **cups water**
2 **packages active dry yeast**
6 **to 6½ cups all-purpose flour**
3 **tablespoons sugar**
2 **tablespoons shortening**
1 **tablespoon salt**
 All-purpose flour *or* cornmeal (optional)

In medium saucepan cook potato in the water about 12 minutes or till tender; *do not drain*. Cool mixture to 110° to 115°. Set aside ½ *cup* of the cooking liquid. Mash potato in the remaining liquid; add enough warm water to make 2 cups potato mixture.

In large mixer bowl soften yeast in the reserved ½ cup potato liquid. Add mashed potato mixture, *2 cups* of the flour, the sugar, shortening, and salt. Beat at low speed of electric mixer for ½ minute, scraping sides of bowl constantly. Beat 3 minutes at high speed.

Stir in as much of the remaining flour as you can mix in with a spoon. Turn out onto lightly floured surface. Knead in enough of the remaining flour to make a moderately stiff dough that is smooth and elastic (6 to 8 minutes total). Shape into a ball. Place in lightly greased bowl; turn once to grease surface. Cover; let rise in warm place till double (about 1 hour).

Punch down; turn out onto lightly floured surface. Divide dough in half. Cover; let rest 10 minutes. Shape each half into a loaf. Place in two greased 8x4x2-inch loaf pans. Cover; let rise till nearly double (about 35 minutes).

If desired, brush tops with a little water and dust lightly with additional flour or cornmeal. Bake in 375° oven for 40 to 45 minutes, covering with foil the last 15 minutes of baking to prevent overbrowning. Remove from pans; cool on wire rack. Makes 2 loaves.

Cornmeal Herb Bread

2 **packages active dry yeast**
½ **cup warm water (110° to 115°)**
1 **teaspoon honey**
1 **cup water**
1 **cup evaporated milk, room temperature**
2 **beaten eggs**
½ **cup honey**
½ **cup cooking oil**
1 **tablespoon salt**
3 **cups whole wheat flour**
3½ **to 4 cups all-purpose flour**
1½ **cups cornmeal**
2 **tablespoons poppy seed**
1 **teaspoon celery seed**
1 **teaspoon dried sage**
1 **teaspoon dried basil, crushed**
½ **teaspoon dried dillweed**
1 **beaten egg yolk**
1 **tablespoon water**
2 **tablespoons sesame seed**

Soften yeast in mixture of the ½ cup warm water and the 1 teaspoon honey for 5 minutes.

In large mixing bowl combine the 1 cup water, evaporated milk, and yeast mixture. Add 2 beaten eggs, ½ cup honey, oil, and salt; mix well. Stir in the whole wheat flour, *2 cups* all-purpose flour, cornmeal, poppy seed, celery seed, sage, basil, and dillweed. Stir in as much of the remaining all-purpose flour as you can mix in with a spoon.

Turn out onto lightly floured surface. Knead in enough of the remaining all-purpose flour to make a moderately stiff dough that is smooth and elastic (6 to 8 minutes total). Shape into a ball. Place in lightly greased bowl; turn once to grease surface. Cover; let rise in warm place till double (about 1¾ hours).

Punch down; turn out onto lightly floured surface. Divide dough in half; shape each half into a ball. Cover; let rest 10 minutes. Shape into loaves; place in two greased 9x5x3-inch loaf pans. Cover; let rise till nearly double (about 40 minutes).

Brush tops of loaves with mixture of beaten egg yolk and 1 tablespoon water. Sprinkle *each* loaf with *1 tablespoon* of the sesame seed. Bake in 375° oven for 30 minutes; cover with foil during the last 15 minutes of baking to prevent overbrowning. Remove from pans. Cool loaves on wire rack. Makes 2 loaves.

Molasses-Oatmeal Bread (pictured on the cover)

5¾ to 6¼ cups all-purpose flour
  2 packages active dry yeast
1¾ cups water
  1 cup quick-cooking rolled oats
  ½ cup light molasses
  ⅓ cup shortening
  1 tablespoon salt
  2 eggs
    Quick-cooking rolled oats
  1 beaten egg white (optional)
  1 tablespoon water (optional)

In large mixer bowl combine 2 cups of the flour and the yeast. In saucepan heat the 1¾ cups water, the 1 cup rolled oats, molasses, shortening, and salt just till warm (115° to 120°) and shortening is almost melted; stir constantly. Add to flour mixture. Add the 2 eggs. Beat at low speed of electric mixer for ½ minute, scraping bowl. Beat 3 minutes at high speed. Stir in as much of the remaining flour as you can mix in with a spoon. Turn out onto lightly floured surface. Knead in enough of the remaining flour to make a moderately soft dough that is smooth and elastic (3 to 5 minutes total). Shape into a ball. Place in lightly greased bowl; turn once to grease surface. Cover; let rise in warm place till double (about 1½ hours).

Punch down; turn out onto lightly floured surface. Divide dough in half. Cover; let rest 10 minutes. Grease two 9x5x3-inch loaf pans. If desired, coat each pan with about 3 tablespoons rolled oats.

Shape dough into loaves. Place loaves in pans. Cover; let rise till nearly double (45 to 60 minutes). If desired, brush loaves with mixture of egg white and 1 tablespoon water; sprinkle tops lightly with additional rolled oats. Bake in 375° oven for 40 to 45 minutes or till done. Cover loosely with foil the last 15 minutes of baking to prevent overbrowning. Remove from pans; cool on wire rack. Makes 2 loaves.

Poppy Seed Loaf

5¼ to 5¾ cups all-purpose flour
  2 packages active dry yeast
1½ cups milk
  ⅓ cup sugar
  ⅓ cup shortening
  1 teaspoon salt
  3 eggs
  1 cup boiling water
  ¾ cup poppy seed
  ½ cup chopped nuts
  ⅓ cup honey
  1 teaspoon finely shredded lemon
    peel
  1 stiff-beaten egg white

In large mixer bowl combine 2 cups of the flour and the yeast. In saucepan heat together milk, sugar, shortening, and salt just till warm (115° to 120°) and shortening is almost melted; stir constantly. Add to flour mixture; add eggs. Beat at low speed of electric mixer for ½ minute, scraping sides of bowl constantly. Beat 3 minutes at high speed. Stir in as much of the remaining flour as you can mix in with a spoon. Turn out onto lightly floured surface. Knead in enough of the remaining flour to make a moderately stiff dough that is smooth and elastic (6 to 8 minutes total). Shape into a ball. Place in lightly greased bowl; turn once to grease surface. Cover; let rise in warm place till double (about 1 hour).

Meanwhile, pour boiling water over poppy seed; let stand 30 minutes. Drain thoroughly. Place poppy seed in blender container; cover and blend till ground. (Or, put through the finest blade of food grinder.) Stir in chopped nuts, honey, and lemon peel. Fold in beaten egg white.

Punch down; divide in half. Cover and let rest 10 minutes. On lightly floured surface, roll half of the dough into a 24x8-inch rectangle; spread with half the poppy seed mixture. Roll up jelly-roll-style, starting with the narrow edge; seal. Place, seam side down, in a greased 8x4x2-inch loaf pan. Repeat with remaining dough and poppy seed mixture. Cover; let rise till nearly double (30 to 45 minutes). Bake in 350° oven for 35 to 40 minutes. Remove from pans; cool on wire rack. Makes 2 loaves.

Sink your teeth into a slice of thick and chewy *Russian Black Bread*. Rye flour,
whole bran, coffee, chocolate, caraway, and fennel all add to the flavor of this hearty loaf.

Russian Black Bread

3½ **to 4 cups all-purpose flour**
  4 **cups rye flour**
  2 **cups whole bran cereal**
  2 **packages active dry yeast**
  2 **tablespoons instant coffee**
    crystals
  2 **tablespoons caraway seed**
  1 **tablespoon sugar**
  1 **tablespoon salt**
  1 **teaspoon fennel seed, crushed**
2½ **cups water**
  ⅓ **cup molasses**
  ¼ **cup butter** *or* **margarine**
  1 **square (1 ounce) unsweetened**
    chocolate
  2 **tablespoons vinegar**
  ½ **cup cold water**
  1 **tablespoon cornstarch**

In large mixer bowl combine *3 cups* of the all-purpose flour, *1 cup* of the rye flour, the whole bran cereal, the yeast, coffee crystals, caraway seed, sugar, salt, and fennel seed. In saucepan heat together the 2½ cups water, molasses, butter or margarine, chocolate, and vinegar just till warm (115° to 120°) and chocolate and butter are almost melted; stir constantly. Add molasses mixture to flour mixture in mixer bowl. Beat at low speed of electric mixer ½ minute, scraping bowl. Beat 3 minutes at high speed. Stir in remaining 3 cups rye flour and as much of the remaining all-purpose flour as you can mix in with a spoon.

Turn out onto lightly floured surface. Knead in enough of the remaining all-purpose flour to make a moderately stiff dough that is smooth and elastic (6 to 8 minutes total). (Dough may be slightly sticky because of the rye flour.) Shape into a ball. Place in lightly greased bowl; turn once to grease surface. Cover; let rise in warm place till nearly double (1¼ to 1½ hours).

Punch down; divide in half. Shape each half into a ball. Place on greased baking sheets. Flatten slightly with palm of hand to 6- to 7-inch diameter. Cover; let rise till nearly double (30 to 45 minutes). Bake in 375° oven for 50 to 60 minutes or till well browned and bread sounds hollow when tapped. Remove from baking sheets; cool on wire rack.

Meanwhile, in small saucepan combine the ½ cup cold water and cornstarch. Cook and stir till thickened and bubbly; cook 1 minute more. Brush over *hot* bread. Makes 2 loaves.

Sausage Bread

  ½ **pound bulk** *or* **link Italian**
    sausage
3¼ **to 3¾ cups all-purpose flour**
  1 **package active dry yeast**
1¼ **cups warm water (115° to 120°)**
  ½ **teaspoon salt**

In skillet cook sausage over medium heat till browned, breaking sausage apart as it cooks. (If using link sausage, remove casings before cooking.) Drain well; set aside.

In large mixer bowl combine *1½ cups* of the flour and the yeast. Combine warm water and salt. Add to flour mixture in mixer bowl. Beat at low speed of electric mixer for ½ minute, scraping bowl constantly. Beat 3 minutes at high speed. Stir in the sausage and as much of the remaining flour as you can mix in with a spoon. Turn out onto lightly floured surface. Knead in enough of the remaining flour to make a moderately stiff dough that is smooth and elastic (6 to 8 minutes total). Shape into a ball. Place dough in lightly greased bowl; turn once to grease surface. Cover; let rise in warm place till double (45 to 60 minutes).

Punch down; turn out onto lightly floured surface. Cover; let rest 10 minutes. Shape into loaf; place in greased 8x4x2-inch loaf pan. Cover; let rise till nearly double (30 to 45 minutes). Bake in 400° oven about 35 minutes or till done. Cover bread with foil after 20 minutes of baking to prevent overbrowning. Remove from pan; cool on wire rack. Makes 1 loaf.

Rye Bread

3¼ to 3¾ cups all-purpose flour
  2 packages active dry yeast
  1 tablespoon caraway seed
  2 cups warm water (115° to 120°)
  ½ cup packed brown sugar
  1 tablespoon cooking oil
  1 teaspoon salt
2½ cups rye flour

In bowl combine *2½ cups* all-purpose flour, the yeast, and caraway. Mix water, brown sugar, oil, and salt. Add to flour mixture. Beat at low speed of electric mixer ½ minute, scraping bowl. Beat 3 minutes at high speed. Stir in rye flour and as much remaining all-purpose flour as you can mix in with a spoon. Turn out onto floured surface. Knead in enough remaining all-purpose flour to make a moderately stiff dough that is smooth and elastic (6 to 8 minutes total). (Dough will be sticky.) Place in greased bowl; turn once. Cover; let rise till double (about 1½ hours).

Punch down; divide in half. Cover; let rest 10 minutes. Shape into two 4½-inch round loaves on greased baking sheets (or, shape and place in two greased 8x4x2-inch loaf pans). Cover; let rise till nearly double (about 40 minutes). Bake in 350° oven 40 to 45 minutes. Cool on wire rack. Makes 2.

Whole Wheat-Raisin-Apple Bread

  2 packages active dry yeast
  ½ cup warm water (110° to 115°)
  1 beaten egg
  1 cup warm milk (115° to 120°)
  ¼ cup honey
1½ teaspoons salt
  1 cup raisins
  1 cup finely chopped, peeled tart
     apple (2 small apples)
2¼ to 2¾ cups all-purpose flour
1½ cups whole wheat flour
  ½ cup cracked wheat
  1 beaten egg yolk
  1 tablespoon water

Soften yeast in the ½ cup warm water. In bowl combine egg, milk, honey, and salt; add yeast mixture, raisins, and apple. In large bowl stir together *1½ cups* of the all-purpose flour and the whole wheat flour; add milk mixture, mixing well. Stir in cracked wheat. Turn out onto lightly floured surface. Knead in enough remaining all-purpose flour to make a moderately stiff dough that is smooth and elastic (6 to 8 minutes total). Place in greased bowl; turn once. Cover; let rise in warm place till double (about 1 hour).

Punch down; divide into three portions. Cover; let rest 10 minutes. Shape into three loaves. Place in three greased 7½x3½x2-inch loaf pans. Cover; let rise till nearly double (30 to 45 minutes). Beat together the egg yolk and 1 tablespoon water; brush over loaves. Bake in 375° oven 30 minutes, covering with foil after the first 15 minutes of baking to prevent overbrowning. Cool on wire racks. Makes 3 loaves.

Peasant Bread

  3 to 3½ cups all-purpose flour
  2 packages active dry yeast
1¾ cups water
  ¼ cup dark molasses
  2 tablespoons cooking oil
  2 teaspoons salt
1½ cups rye flour
  ½ cup whole bran cereal
  ⅓ cup yellow cornmeal
  1 tablespoon caraway seed

In bowl combine *2 cups* all-purpose flour and the yeast. Heat water, molasses, oil, and salt just till warm (115° to 120°); stir constantly. Add to flour mixture. Beat at low speed of electric mixer ½ minute, scraping bowl. Beat 3 minutes at high speed. Stir in rye flour, bran, cornmeal, caraway, and as much remaining all-purpose flour as you can mix in with a spoon. Turn out onto lightly floured surface. Knead in enough remaining all-purpose flour to make a moderately stiff dough that is smooth and elastic (6 to 8 minutes total). Shape into a ball. Place in greased bowl; turn once. Cover; let rise till double (1 to 1¼ hours).

Punch down; turn out onto floured surface. Divide in half. Cover; let rest 10 minutes. Shape into 2 loaves; place in two greased 8x4x2-inch loaf pans. Cover; let rise till nearly double (30 to 45 minutes). Bake in 375° oven 35 to 40 minutes or till done. Cool on wire rack. Makes 2 loaves.

Challah

7 to 7½ cups all-purpose flour
2 packages active dry yeast
2 cups water
¼ cup sugar
¼ cup pareve margarine, butter, *or*
    margarine
2 teaspoons salt
3 eggs
1 egg yolk
1 tablespoon water
    Poppy seed

In large mixer bowl combine *3 cups* of the flour and the yeast. In saucepan heat together the 2 cups water; sugar; pareve margarine, butter, or margarine; and salt just till warm (115° to 120°) and butter is almost melted; stir constantly. Add to flour mixture; add 3 eggs. Beat at low speed of electric mixer ½ minute, scraping bowl. Beat 3 minutes at high speed. Stir in as much of the remaining flour as you can mix in with a spoon. Turn out onto lightly floured surface. Knead in enough of the remaining flour to make a moderately stiff dough that is smooth and elastic (6 to 8 minutes total). Place in lightly greased bowl; turn once. Cover; let rise in warm place till double (about 45 minutes).

Punch down; divide dough into 3 portions. Divide each portion into 3 pieces. Cover; let rest 10 minutes. Roll each piece into a 16-inch rope. Using three ropes for each loaf, braid and secure ends, forming 3 loaves. Place on greased baking sheets. Cover; let rise till nearly double (about 35 minutes). Brush with mixture of egg yolk and the 1 tablespoon water. Sprinkle with poppy seed. Bake in 375° oven 25 to 30 minutes or till lightly browned. Remove from baking sheets. Cool on wire racks. Makes 3 loaves.

Pinwheel Bread

2 packages active dry yeast
2 cups warm water (110° to 115°)
2 cups milk
½ cup sugar
½ cup shortening
2 tablespoons salt
8¼ to 8¾ cups all-purpose flour
¼ cup molasses
4 to 4½ cups whole wheat flour

In large mixing bowl dissolve yeast in warm water. In saucepan heat together milk, sugar, shortening, and salt just till warm (110° to 115°) and shortening is almost melted; stir constantly. Add to yeast mixture. Stir in *4 cups* of the all-purpose flour; beat till smooth. Cover; let rise in warm place 1 hour. Stir batter down. Turn *half* of the batter (about 4 cups) into another mixing bowl. To one half of batter, stir in as much remaining all-purpose flour as you can mix in with a spoon. Turn out onto lightly floured surface. Knead in enough remaining all-purpose flour to make a moderately stiff dough that is smooth and elastic (6 to 8 minutes total). Shape into a ball. Place in greased bowl; turn once. Cover.

To remaining half of batter, stir in molasses till well combined. Stir in as much of the whole wheat flour as you can mix in with a spoon. Turn out onto lightly floured surface. Knead in enough of the remaining whole wheat flour to make a moderately stiff dough that is smooth and elastic (6 to 8 minutes total). Place in lightly greased bowl; turn once to grease surface. Cover. Let both doughs rise till double (45 to 60 minutes).

Punch doughs down; let rest 10 minutes. Divide each half of dough into 3 portions. On lightly floured surface, roll out each portion of dough to a 12x8-inch rectangle. Place one dark portion of dough atop one light portion. Roll up tightly into a loaf, starting with narrow edge. Place loaf in greased 9x5x3-inch loaf pan. Repeat with remaining portions to make 3 loaves. Cover; let rise till nearly double (45 to 60 minutes). Bake in 375° oven 30 to 35 minutes. Cover with foil after 20 minutes of baking to prevent overbrowning. Remove from pans. Cool on wire racks. Makes 3 loaves.

Yeast Rolls

Dinner Rolls

4 to 4½ cups all-purpose flour
1 package active dry yeast
1 cup milk
⅓ cup sugar
⅓ cup butter, margarine, *or*
    shortening
1 teaspoon salt
2 eggs

This basic yeast roll dough also can be used to make Basic Sweet Rolls (see recipe on page 34).

In large mixer bowl combine *2 cups* of the flour and the yeast. In saucepan heat milk; sugar; butter, margarine, or shortening; and salt just till warm (115° to 120°) and butter is almost melted; stir constantly. Add to flour mixture; add eggs. Beat at low speed of electric mixer for ½ minute, scraping sides of bowl constantly. Beat 3 minutes at high speed.

Stir in as much of the remaining flour as you can mix in with a spoon. Turn out onto a lightly floured surface. Knead in enough of the remaining flour to make a moderately stiff dough that is smooth and elastic (6 to 8 minutes total). Shape into a ball. Place in lightly greased bowl; turn once to grease surface. Cover; let rise in warm place till double (about 1 hour).

Punch down; divide dough in half. Cover; let rest 10 minutes. Shape into desired rolls (see below and illustrations at right). Cover; let rise till nearly double (about 30 minutes). Bake in 375° oven for 12 to 15 minutes or till done. Makes 2 to 2½ dozen.

Brown-and-Serve Rolls: Prepare Dinner Rolls as directed above. Shape into desired rolls as directed below and as illustrated at right. Cover; let rise till nearly double (about 30 minutes). Bake in 325° oven about 10 minutes; *do not brown*. Remove from pans; cool. Wrap, label, and freeze.

To serve, open packages containing desired number of rolls. Thaw rolls in package at room temperature for 10 to 15 minutes. Unwrap completely. Bake on ungreased baking sheets in 400° oven about 10 minutes or till golden. Serve warm.

Hamburger Buns: Prepare Dinner Rolls as directed above; let rise till double. Punch dough down; divide into 12 portions. Cover; let rest 10 minutes. Shape each into an even circle, folding edges under. Press flat between hands. Place on greased baking sheet; press to 3½-inch circles. Cover; let rise till nearly double (about 30 minutes). Bake in 375° oven for 12 to 15 minutes or till golden. Remove rolls from sheet; cool on wire racks. Makes 12 buns.

Frankfurter Buns: Prepare Dinner Rolls as directed above; let rise till double. Punch dough down; divide into 12 portions. Cover; let rest 10 minutes. Shape into rolls about 5½ inches long, tapering ends. Place on greased baking sheet. Cover; let rise till nearly double (about 30 minutes). Bake in 375° oven for 12 to 15 minutes or till golden. Remove rolls from sheet; cool on wire racks. Makes 12 buns.

To make Shortcut Cloverleaves, lightly grease 24 muffin cups. Divide each *half* of dough into 12 pieces. Shape each piece into a ball, pulling edges under to make a smooth top. Place one ball in each greased muffin cup, smooth side up.

Using scissors dipped in flour, snip top in half, then snip again to make 4 points, as shown. Let rise and bake as directed. Makes 24.

To make Cloverleaves, lightly grease 24 muffin cups. Divide each *half* of dough into 36 pieces. Shape each piece into a ball, pulling edges under to make a smooth top. Place 3 balls in each greased muffin cup, smooth side up, as shown. Let rise and bake as directed. Makes 24.

To make Butterhorns, lightly grease baking sheets. On lightly floured surface, roll each *half* of dough into a 12-inch circle. Brush with melted *butter*. Cut each circle into 12 wedges. To shape, begin at wide end of wedge and roll toward point, as shown. Place, point down, 2 to 3 inches apart on baking sheets. Let rise and bake as directed. Makes 24.

To make Parker House Rolls, lightly grease baking sheets. On lightly floured surface, roll out each *half* of dough to ¼-inch thickness. Cut with floured 2½-inch round cutter. Brush with melted *butter*. Make an off-center crease in each round. Fold so large half overlaps slightly, as shown. Place 2 to 3 inches apart on baking sheets. Let rise and bake as directed. Makes 30.

To make Rosettes, lightly grease baking sheets. Divide each *half* of dough into 16 pieces. On lightly floured surface, roll each into a 12-inch rope. Tie in a loose knot, leaving two long ends. Tuck top end under roll. Bring bottom end up; tuck into center of roll, as shown. Place 2 to 3 inches apart on baking sheets. Let rise and bake as directed. Makes 32.

Reheating Yeast Rolls

• To reheat rolls in the oven, place rolls in a brown paper bag; sprinkle bag with water (a clothes sprinkler works well) and fold the opening closed. Heat rolls in a 325° oven for about 10 minutes or till heated through. Or, reheat rolls in foil, sprinkling rolls with water before wrapping.

• To reheat rolls in a countertop microwave oven, place rolls on a paper napkin or paper plate to absorb moisture. Heat 1 roll on high power for 10 to 15 seconds; 2 rolls for 15 to 20 seconds; or 4 rolls for 25 to 30 seconds.

Croissants (pictured on pages 6 and 7)

1½ **cups butter *or* margarine**
⅓ **cup all-purpose flour**
2 **packages active dry yeast**
½ **cup warm water (110° to 115°)**
¾ **cup milk**
¼ **cup sugar**
1 **teaspoon salt**
1 **egg**
3¾ **to 4¼ cups all-purpose flour**
1 **egg yolk**
1 **tablespoon milk**

Cream butter or margarine with ⅓ cup flour. Roll butter mixture between two sheets of waxed paper into a 12x6-inch rectangle. Chill at least 1 hour.

Soften yeast in warm water. Heat ¾ cup milk, sugar, and salt till sugar dissolves. Cool to lukewarm; turn into large mixing bowl. Add softened yeast and 1 egg; beat well.

Stir in *2 cups* of the flour; beat well. Stir in as much of the remaining flour as you can mix in with a spoon. Turn dough out onto lightly floured surface. Knead in enough of the remaining flour to make a moderately soft dough that is smooth and elastic (3 to 5 minutes total). Cover; let rest 10 minutes.

Roll dough into a 14-inch square. Place *chilled* butter on one half of dough; fold over other half and seal edges. Roll into a 21x12-inch rectangle. Chill dough. Fold into thirds; seal edges. Roll into a 21x12-inch rectangle. Fold and roll twice more. Chill after each rolling. Fold into thirds to 12x7 inches. Chill several hours or overnight.

Cut dough crosswise into fourths. Roll each fourth into a 12-inch circle. Cut each into 12 wedges. Roll up each wedge loosely, starting from the side opposite the point.

Place, point down, on ungreased baking sheets; curve ends. Cover; let rise till nearly double (30 to 45 minutes). Beat egg yolk with 1 tablespoon milk; brush over rolls. Bake in 375° oven for 12 to 15 minutes or till golden. Remove from baking sheets. Serve warm. Makes 48 rolls.

Pull-Apart Onion Rolls

2¼ **to 2¾ cups all-purpose flour**
1 **package active dry yeast**
¾ **cup milk**
2 **tablespoons butter *or* margarine**
1 **tablespoon sugar**
½ **teaspoon salt**
1 **egg**
2 **teaspoons minced dried onion**
2 **teaspoons water**
3 **tablespoons butter *or* margarine, melted**
1 **tablespoon grated parmesan cheese**
1 **tablespoon sesame seed**
½ **teaspoon paprika**
¼ **teaspoon garlic salt**

In large mixer bowl combine *1 cup* of the flour and the yeast. In saucepan heat together milk, 2 tablespoons butter or margarine, sugar, and salt just till warm (115° to 120°) and butter is almost melted, stirring constantly. Add to flour mixture in bowl; add egg. Beat at low speed of electric mixer for ½ minute, scraping sides of bowl constantly. Beat 3 minutes at high speed. Stir in as much of the remaining flour as you can mix in with a spoon. Turn out onto lightly floured surface. Knead in enough of the remaining flour to make a moderately stiff dough that is smooth and elastic (6 to 8 minutes total). Shape into a ball. Place in lightly greased bowl; turn once. Cover; let rise in warm place till double (about 45 minutes). Punch down. Cover; let rest 10 minutes.

Meanwhile, prepare onion butter. In bowl combine minced dried onion and water; let stand 5 minutes. Stir in the 3 tablespoons melted butter or margarine, parmesan cheese, sesame seed, paprika, and garlic salt.

Roll dough into an 8-inch square. Spread with onion butter. Cut into sixteen 2-inch squares. Arrange squares, onion side up, in greased 1½-quart casserole, layering as necessary to fit. Cover; let rise till nearly double (about 45 minutes). Bake in 350° oven for 25 to 30 minutes, covering with foil after first 15 minutes of baking to prevent over-browning. Cool in dish 5 minutes; carefully turn out. Serve warm. Makes 16 rolls.

Batter Rolls

3¼ cups all-purpose flour
1 package active dry yeast
1¼ cups milk
½ cup shortening
¼ cup sugar
1 teaspoon salt
1 egg
  Milk
1 tablespoon poppy seed *or*
  sesame seed (optional)

In mixer bowl combine *2 cups* of the flour and the yeast. Heat milk, shortening, sugar, and salt just till warm (115° to 120°) and shortening is almost melted; stir constantly. Add to flour mixture; add egg. Beat at low speed of electric mixer for ½ minute, scraping bowl. Beat 3 minutes at high speed. Add remaining flour; beat at low speed about 2 minutes or till batter is smooth.

Cover; let rise in warm place till double (about 1 hour). Beat down with wooden spoon. Let rest 5 minutes. Spoon into greased muffin cups, filling each half full. Cover; let rise till nearly double (about 30 minutes). Brush tops lightly with milk; sprinkle with poppy or sesame seed, if desired. Bake in 375° oven 15 to 18 minutes. Makes 18 rolls.

Cornmeal Buns

5¾ to 6¼ cups all-purpose flour
1 package active dry yeast
2¼ cups milk
½ cup sugar
½ cup butter *or* margarine
1 teaspoon salt
2 eggs
1½ cups yellow cornmeal

In mixer bowl combine *3 cups* of the flour and the yeast. Heat milk, sugar, butter, and salt just till warm (115° to 120°) and butter is almost melted; stir constantly. Add to flour mixture; add eggs. Beat at low speed of electric mixer for ½ minute, scraping bowl. Beat 3 minutes at high speed. Add cornmeal; beat at low speed. Stir in as much of the remaining flour as you can mix in with a spoon. Turn out onto lightly floured surface. Knead in enough of the remaining flour to make a moderately stiff dough that is smooth and elastic (6 to 8 minutes total). Shape into a ball. Place in greased bowl; turn once to grease surface. Cover; let rise in warm place till double (1 to 1¼ hours). Punch down; turn out onto lightly floured surface. Cover; let rest 10 minutes. Shape into 72 balls; place 2 in each of 36 greased muffin cups. Cover; let rise till nearly double (50 to 60 minutes). Bake in 375° oven 12 to 15 minutes. Makes 36 buns.

Rye Rolls (pictured on page 26)

2½ to 3 cups all-purpose flour
2 packages active dry yeast
2 tablespoons caraway seed
2 cups milk
½ cup sugar
3 tablespoons shortening
1 tablespoon salt
2 eggs
4 cups rye flour
1 slightly beaten egg white
1 tablespoon water
  Coarse salt (optional)

In mixer bowl combine *2 cups* all-purpose flour, the yeast, and caraway. Heat milk, sugar, shortening, and salt just till warm (115° to 120°) and shortening is almost melted; stir constantly. Add to flour mixture; add eggs. Beat at low speed of electric mixer for ½ minute, scraping bowl. Beat 3 minutes at high speed. Stir in the rye flour and as much of the remaining all-purpose flour as you can mix in with a spoon. Turn out onto lightly floured surface. Knead in enough of the remaining all-purpose flour to make a moderately stiff dough that is smooth and elastic (6 to 8 minutes total). Shape into a ball. Place in greased bowl; turn once to grease surface. Cover; let rise in warm place till double (about 1¼ hours).

Punch down; let rest 10 minutes. Shape into 24 oval-shaped rolls. Place on greased baking sheets. Cover; let rise till nearly double (45 to 60 minutes). Brush with mixture of egg white and water; sprinkle with coarse salt, if desired. Bake in 375° oven for 15 to 20 minutes. Makes 24.

Yeast rolls offer a variety of shapes and flavors. Pictured from the top are egg- and butter-rich *Brioche*, salted *Rye Rolls* (see recipe, page 25), and crescent-shaped *Whole Wheat Butterhorns*.

Whole Wheat Butterhorns

2½ to 3 cups all-purpose flour
2 packages active dry yeast
1¾ cups water
⅓ cup packed brown sugar
3 tablespoons shortening
2 tablespoons honey
2 teaspoons salt
2 cups whole wheat flour
6 tablespoons butter or
　margarine, softened
½ cup very finely chopped filberts
　Butter or margarine, melted

In large mixer bowl combine 1½ cups of the all-purpose flour and the yeast. In saucepan heat water, brown sugar, shortening, honey, and salt just till warm (115° to 120°) and shortening is almost melted; stir constantly. Add to flour mixture. Beat at low speed of electric mixer for ½ minute, scraping sides of bowl constantly. Beat 3 minutes at high speed. Stir in the whole wheat flour and as much of the remaining all-purpose flour as you can mix in with a spoon. Turn out onto lightly floured surface. Knead in enough of the remaining all-purpose flour to make a moderately stiff dough that is smooth and elastic (6 to 8 minutes total). Shape into a ball. Place dough in a lightly greased bowl; turn once to grease surface. Cover and let rise in warm place till double (about 1½ hours).

Punch down; turn out onto lightly floured surface. Divide dough into 3 equal portions; shape each into a ball. Cover and let rest 10 minutes.

On lightly floured surface, roll one ball of dough into a 12-inch circle; spread with 2 tablespoons of the softened butter and sprinkle with ⅓ of the nuts. Cut circle into 12 wedges. To shape rolls, begin at wide end of wedge and roll toward point. Place, point down, 2 to 3 inches apart on greased baking sheet. Repeat with remaining dough; spread with softened butter and sprinkle with nuts. Cover rolls; let rise in warm place till nearly double (20 to 30 minutes). Brush with melted butter. Bake in 400° oven for 10 to 12 minutes or till done. Remove from baking sheet; cool. Brush again with melted butter, if desired. Makes 36.

Brioche

1 package active dry yeast
¼ cup warm water (110° to 115°)
½ cup butter or margarine
⅓ cup sugar
½ teaspoon salt
4 cups all-purpose flour
½ cup milk
4 eggs
1 tablespoon water

Soften yeast in ¼ cup warm water. Cream butter, sugar, and salt. Add 1 cup of the flour and the milk to creamed mixture. Separate one of the eggs; set egg white aside. Blend yolk with remaining 3 eggs; add to creamed mixture. Add softened yeast; beat well. Stir in the remaining flour till smooth. Turn into greased bowl. Cover; let rise in warm place till double (about 2 hours). Refrigerate overnight; stir down. Turn out onto lightly floured surface. Divide dough into quarters; set one aside. Divide each of the remaining quarters into 8 pieces, making a total of 24. With floured hands, form each piece into a ball, tucking under edges. Place each in a greased muffin cup. Divide reserved dough into 24 pieces; shape into balls.

With floured finger, make an indentation in each large ball. Press a small ball into each indentation. Blend reserved egg white and 1 tablespoon water; brush over rolls. Cover; let rise till nearly double (40 to 45 minutes). Bake in 375° oven about 15 minutes, brushing again after 7 minutes. Makes 24.

To use individual brioche pans, prepare dough and divide into quarters as above; set one aside. Divide each remaining quarter into 6 pieces, making a total of 18. Form into balls; place in 18 greased, individual brioche pans. Divide reserved dough into 18 pieces; shape into balls and place one atop each larger ball. Let rise; bake as directed. Makes 18.

Soft Pretzels   (pictured on pages 6 and 7)

   4 **to 4½ cups all-purpose flour**
   1 **package active dry yeast**
1½ **cups milk**
   ¼ **cup sugar**
   2 **tablespoons cooking oil**
1½ **teaspoons salt**
   3 **tablespoons salt**
   2 **quarts boiling water**
   1 **slightly beaten egg white**
      Sesame seed *or* coarse salt

In mixer bowl combine *2 cups* of the flour and the yeast. In saucepan heat milk, sugar, oil, and 1½ teaspoons salt just till warm (115° to 120°); stir constantly. Add to flour mixture. Beat at low speed of electric mixer for ½ minute, scraping bowl. Beat 3 minutes at high speed. Stir in as much of the remaining flour as you can mix in with a spoon. Turn out onto lightly floured surface. Knead in enough of the remaining flour to make a moderately stiff dough that is smooth and elastic (6 to 8 minutes total). Shape into a ball. Place in lightly greased bowl; turn once to grease surface. Cover; let rise in warm place till double (about 1½ hours).

Punch down; turn out onto lightly floured surface. Cover; let rest 10 minutes. Roll into a 12x8-inch rectangle. Cut into 16 strips, each 12 inches long and ½ inch wide. Roll each into a rope 16 inches long. Shape into pretzels, following directions in tip box below. Let rise, uncovered, 20 minutes. Dissolve 3 tablespoons salt in the boiling water. Lower 3 or 4 pretzels at a time into boiling water; boil for 2 minutes, turning once. Remove with slotted spoon to paper toweling; let stand a few seconds, then place ½ inch apart on well-greased baking sheet. Brush with mixture of egg white and 1 tablespoon *water*. Sprinkle lightly with sesame seed or coarse salt. Bake in 350° oven 25 to 30 minutes or till golden brown. Makes 16 pretzels.

Shaping Pretzels

Shaping a piece of dough into a pretzel isn't difficult, but it may take a couple practice twists to master the technique.

Start by shaping one rope of dough into a circle, overlapping about 4 inches from each end and leaving ends free. Take one end of dough in each hand and twist at the point where dough overlaps.

Carefully lift ends across to the opposite edge of circle, as shown at left. Tuck ends under edge to make a pretzel shape; moisten and press ends to seal.

Pita Bread (pictured on pages 6 and 7)

1 **package active dry yeast**
1¼ **cups warm water (110° to 115°)**
3¼ **to 3¾ cups all-purpose flour**
¼ **cup shortening**
1½ **teaspoons salt**

In large mixer bowl soften yeast in warm water. Add *2 cups* of the flour, the shortening, and salt. Beat at low speed of electric mixer for ½ minute, scraping sides of bowl. Beat 3 minutes at high speed. Stir in as much of the remaining flour as you can mix in with a spoon. Turn out onto lightly floured surface. Knead in enough of the remaining flour to make a moderately soft dough that is smooth and elastic (3 to 5 minutes total). Cover; let rest in a warm place about 15 minutes. Divide into 12 equal portions. Roll each between floured hands into *very* smooth balls. Cover with plastic wrap or a damp cloth; let rest 10 minutes. Using fingers, gently flatten balls without creasing dough. Cover; let rest 10 minutes. (Keep dough pieces covered till ready to use.)

On well-floured surface lightly roll one piece of dough at a time into a 7-inch round, *turning dough over once*. Do not stretch, puncture, or crease dough. Work with enough flour so dough does not stick. Place on a baking sheet.

Bake two at a time in 450° oven about 3 minutes or till dough is puffed and softly set. Turn over with spatula; bake about 2 minutes more or till dough begins to lightly brown. Repeat with remaining dough, baking one batch before rolling and baking the next batch.

To serve, slice bread in half crosswise and generously fill each pocket with desired filling. (Allow any extra bread to just cool before wrapping for storage.) Makes 12 pita rounds.

Whole Wheat Pita Bread: Prepare Pita Bread as above, *except* substitute 2 cups *whole wheat flour* and 1¼ to 1¾ cups *all-purpose flour* for the 3¼ to 3¾ cups all-purpose flour.

Party Pita Bread: Prepare Pita Bread as above, *except* divide the dough into 24 equal portions. Roll into 4-inch rounds and bake about 2 minutes on each side. To serve, slice bread part way along one side and fill with desired filling.

Filling Pita Bread

Think of pita bread simply as two slices of bread fastened together pocket-style and ready to be filled with your favorite cold or hot sandwich filling. Remember, though, that the pita is thinner than bread; if you spoon in too much of a soft salad-type filling or a hot, juicy meat filling, the bread will soak it up and tear.

For starters, put your imagination to work and try a combination of any of the following: crisp-fried bacon; strips or chunks of luncheon meats, chilled cooked ham, roast beef, chicken, or turkey; canned tuna, shrimp, or salmon; sliced hard-cooked eggs; sliced or shredded cheese; shredded carrots, lettuce, or cabbage; chopped onion, celery, green pepper, apple, sunflower seeds, or nuts; bean or alfalfa sprouts; or sliced radishes, olives, mushrooms, tomatoes, or avocado.

Bagels

4¼ to 4¾ cups all-purpose flour
  2 packages active dry yeast
1½ cups warm water (110° to 115°)
  3 tablespoons sugar
  1 tablespoon salt
  1 tablespoon sugar

In mixer bowl combine *1½ cups* of the flour and the yeast. Combine warm water, the 3 tablespoons sugar, and salt. Pour over flour mixture. Beat at low speed of electric mixer ½ minute, scraping bowl. Beat 3 minutes at high speed. Stir in as much remaining flour as you can mix in with a spoon.

Turn out onto lightly floured surface. Knead in enough remaining flour to make a moderately stiff dough that is smooth and elastic (6 to 8 minutes total). Cover; let rest 10 minutes. Cut into 12 portions; shape each into a smooth ball. Punch a hole in center of each (step 1). Pull gently to make a 1½- to 2-inch hole (step 2). Place on greased baking sheet. Cover; let rise 20 minutes. Broil 5 inches from heat 3 to 4 minutes, turning once (tops should not brown). Heat 1 gallon *water* and the 1 tablespoon sugar to boiling; reduce heat. Cook 4 or 5 bagels at a time for 7 minutes, turning once; drain (step 3). Place on greased baking sheet. Bake in 375° oven 25 to 30 minutes. Makes 12.

Light Rye Bagels: Prepare as above, *except* substitute 1¼ cups *rye flour* for 1¼ cups of the all-purpose flour.

Whole Wheat Bagels: Prepare Bagels as above, *except* substitute 1¼ cups *whole wheat flour* for 1¼ cups of the all-purpose flour.

Herb Bagels: Prepare Bagels as above, *except* add 2 teaspoons dried *marjoram*, crushed; *or* 1 teaspoon dried *dillweed*; *or* 1 teaspoon dried *tarragon*, crushed; *or* ½ teaspoon *garlic powder* to the flour-yeast mixture.

Parmesan Bagels: Prepare Bagels as above, *except* stir ¼ cup grated *parmesan cheese* into the flour-yeast mixture.

Onion Bagels: Prepare Bagels as above. Cook ½ cup finely chopped *onion* in 3 tablespoons *butter or margarine* till tender but not brown. Brush onion-butter mixture over tops of bagels after first 15 minutes of baking.

Poppy Seed or Sesame Seed Bagels: Prepare Bagels as above. Before baking, brush tops with beaten *egg*; sprinkle with *poppy seed* or toasted *sesame seed*.

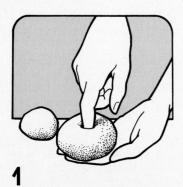

1

Cut dough into 12 equal portions; shape into smooth balls. Punch a hole in the center of each with a floured finger, as shown.

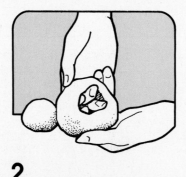

2

Pull dough gently to make a 1½- to 2-inch hole, as shown. While pulling, try to keep bagels uniformly shaped.

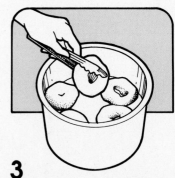

3

Heat 1 gallon *water* and the 1 tablespoon sugar to boiling; reduce heat to simmering. Cook 4 or 5 bagels at a time for 7 minutes, turning once; drain on paper toweling.

Shape, broil, boil, and bake are the easy steps to making *Bagels*. For variety, use whole wheat or rye flours, add an herb or parmesan cheese, or top with onions, poppy seed, or sesame seed.

English Muffins

5½ to 6 cups all-purpose flour
 2 packages active dry yeast
 2 cups milk
 2 tablespoons sugar
 2 tablespoons shortening
 2 teaspoons salt
   Cornmeal

In mixer bowl stir together *2 cups* of the flour and the yeast. In saucepan heat milk, sugar, shortening, and salt till warm (115° to 120°) and shortening is almost melted, stirring constantly. Add to flour mixture. Beat at low speed of electric mixer for ½ minute, scraping sides of bowl constantly. Beat at high speed for 3 minutes. Stir in as much of the remaining flour as you can mix in with a spoon.

Turn out onto lightly floured surface. Knead in enough of the remaining flour to make a moderately stiff dough that is smooth and elastic (6 to 8 minutes total). Place dough in greased bowl; turn once to grease surface. Cover; let rise in warm place till double (about 1¼ hours).

Punch down; cover and let rest 10 minutes. On lightly floured surface, roll out dough to about ¼-inch thickness. Cut with a 4-inch round cutter. Dip in cornmeal to coat both sides. Cover; let rise till very light (about 30 minutes).

Place 4 muffins on each of 4 ungreased *griddles or skillets*. Cook over medium heat for 25 minutes; turn frequently. Cool. Split; toast both sides. Makes 16.

If you don't have four skillets, cook only *half* of the dough at a time. Cover the remaining dough and keep refrigerated. If desired, cut the remaining dough before refrigerating. The cut muffins will rise slightly while in the refrigerator, so they may not need all of the suggested 30 minutes to rise and become light.

Whole Wheat English Muffins: Prepare as above, *except* combine yeast with ¾ cup all-purpose flour, 1½ cups *whole wheat flour*, ½ cup *cracked wheat*, and ¼ cup *wheat germ*. Increase shortening to ¼ *cup*. Use up to 2½ cups all-purpose flour as the remaining amount to be stirred and kneaded into dough. Makes 12 muffins.

Ham-and-Cheese Brunch Rolls

3¼ to 3¾ cups all-purpose flour
 1 package active dry yeast
1¼ cups milk
 ¼ cup shortening
 ¼ cup sugar
 1 teaspoon salt
 1 egg
 ¾ cup finely chopped fully cooked
   ham
 ½ cup shredded cheddar cheese
   (2 ounces)
   Butter *or* margarine, melted

In mixer bowl combine *2 cups* of the flour and the yeast. Heat milk, shortening, sugar, and salt just till warm (115° to 120°) and shortening is almost melted; stir constantly. Add to flour mixture; add egg. Beat at low speed of electric mixer for ½ minute, scraping sides of bowl. Beat 3 minutes at high speed. Stir in as much of the remaining flour as you can mix in with a spoon.

Turn out onto lightly floured surface. Knead in enough of the remaining flour to make a moderately stiff dough that is smooth and elastic (6 to 8 minutes total). Shape into a ball. Place in greased bowl; turn once to grease surface. Cover; let rise in warm place till double (about 1 hour).

Punch down. Cover; let rest 10 minutes. On lightly floured surface, roll dough to ¾-inch thickness. Using a 2½-inch round cutter, cut into circles. Combine ham and cheese for filling; place *2 teaspoons* mixture in center of each circle. Shape dough around filling, forming into balls. Place each into greased muffin cup. Brush with melted butter or margarine. Cover; let rise till nearly double (about 1 hour). Bake in 400° oven 15 to 20 minutes. Makes 18.

Breadsticks

2 to 2½ cups all-purpose flour
1 package active dry yeast
¾ cup milk
2 tablespoons shortening
1 tablespoon sugar
1 teaspoon salt
1 egg white (optional)
1 tablespoon water (optional)
  Coarse salt, sesame seed, *or*
  poppy seed (optional)

In small mixer bowl combine ¾ *cup* of the flour and the yeast. In saucepan heat milk, shortening, sugar, and salt just till warm (115° to 120°) and shortening is almost melted, stirring constantly. Add to flour mixture. Beat at low speed of electric mixer for ½ minute, scraping sides of bowl constantly. Beat 3 minutes at high speed. Stir in as much of the remaining flour as you can mix in with a spoon. Turn out onto lightly floured surface. Knead in enough of the remaining flour to make a stiff dough that is smooth and elastic (8 to 10 minutes total). Shape into a ball. Place in lightly greased bowl; turn once to grease surface. Cover; let rise in warm place till double (45 to 60 minutes).

Punch down; turn out onto lightly floured surface. Divide dough into 4 portions. Cover; let rest 10 minutes. Divide each portion into 6 pieces. Roll each piece into a rope 8 inches long. Place on greased baking sheets. Cover; let rise in warm place till nearly double (about 30 minutes). If desired, brush with a mixture of the egg white and water, and sprinkle with coarse salt, sesame seed, or poppy seed.

Bake in 375° oven for 10 to 15 minutes or till golden brown. (For drier breadsticks, after baking 10 minutes, decrease oven temperature to 300° and bake 25 to 30 minutes longer.) Makes 24 breadsticks.

Parmesan Breadsticks: Prepare Breadsticks as above, *except* stir ⅓ cup grated *parmesan cheese* into the ¾ cup flour and yeast. Omit sprinkling with coarse salt or seeds.

Barbecue Breadsticks: Prepare Breadstick dough as above, *except* decrease the milk to ⅔ *cup* and stir 2 tablespoons bottled *barbecue sauce* and 1 teaspoon *minced dried onion* into the milk-shortening mixture in saucepan. Omit sprinkling breadsticks with coarse salt or seeds. For drier barbecue breadsticks, bake in 375° oven for 10 minutes; decrease temperature to 300° and bake only 15 to 20 minutes longer.

Pizza Twists

1 13¾-ounce package hot roll mix
1 egg
1 teaspoon minced dried onion
1 cup finely chopped pepperoni (4 ounces)
½ cup shredded cheddar cheese (2 ounces)
1 tablespoon grated parmesan cheese
½ teaspoon dried oregano, crushed
⅛ teaspoon garlic powder
1 beaten egg yolk
1 tablespoon water

Soften yeast from hot roll mix according to package directions. Stir in the egg and minced dried onion. Combine flour mixture from the hot roll mix with the pepperoni, cheddar cheese, parmesan cheese, oregano, and garlic powder. Stir into yeast mixture; mix well. Turn out onto lightly floured surface and knead till smooth (about 5 minutes). Place in lightly greased bowl; turn once to grease surface. Cover and let rise in warm place till double (about 1 hour).

Punch down; turn out onto lightly floured surface. Cut into 24 portions; roll each into a rope 10 inches long. Fold rope in half; twist two or three times. Seal ends with a little water. Place on greased baking sheets. Combine egg yolk and water; brush over rolls. Cover; let rise till nearly double (30 to 45 minutes). Bake in 400° oven for 12 to 15 minutes or till lightly browned. Remove rolls from baking sheets; cool on wire racks. Makes 24 rolls.

Sweet Rolls, Doughnuts, and Coffee Cakes

Basic Sweet Rolls

4 to 4½ cups all-purpose flour
1 package active dry yeast
1 cup milk
⅓ cup sugar
**⅓ cup butter, margarine, *or*
  shortening**
1 teaspoon salt
2 eggs

This basic yeast roll dough also can be used in making dinner rolls and hamburger and frankfurter buns (see recipe, page 22).

In mixer bowl combine *2 cups* flour and the yeast. Heat milk, sugar, butter, and salt just till warm (115° to 120°); stir constantly. Add to flour mixture; add eggs. Beat at low speed of electric mixer for ½ minute. Beat 3 minutes at high speed. Stir in as much of the remaining flour as you can mix in with a spoon. On floured surface, knead in enough of remaining flour to make a moderately stiff dough that is smooth and elastic (6 to 8 minutes total). Shape into a ball in greased bowl; turn once. Cover; let rise in warm place till double (about 1 hour). Punch down; divide in half. Cover; let rest 10 minutes. Shape and bake as below, referring to illustrations at right. Makes 24 rolls.

Creamy Cinnamon Rolls: Prepare Basic Sweet Roll dough as directed. Divide dough in half. Roll one *half* into a 12x8-inch rectangle. Melt 3 tablespoons *butter;* brush *half* over dough (step 1). Combine ⅔ cup packed *brown sugar,* ½ cup chopped *walnuts,* and 2 teaspoons *ground cinnamon;* sprinkle *half* over dough. Roll up jelly-roll-style, beginning from longest side (step 2). Seal seams (step 3). Slice into 12 pieces (step 4). Place in greased 9x1½-inch round baking pan. Repeat with remaining. Cover; let rise till nearly double (about 30 minutes). Pour a total of ¾ cup *whipping cream* over two pans (step 5). Bake in 375° oven 20 to 25 minutes. Cool slightly; invert onto serving plate.

Caramel-Pecan Rolls: Prepare Basic Sweet Roll dough as directed. Divide dough in half. Roll one *half* into a 12x8-inch rectangle. Melt 3 tablespoons *butter or margarine;* brush *half* over dough (step 1). Combine ½ cup granulated *sugar* and 1 teaspoon *ground cinnamon;* sprinkle *half* over dough. Roll up jelly-roll-style, beginning from longest side (step 2). Seal seams (step 3). Cut into 12 pieces (step 4). Repeat with remaining dough. In saucepan combine ⅔ cup packed *brown sugar,* ¼ cup *butter,* and 2 tablespoons *light corn syrup;* cook and stir till blended. Divide between two 9x1½-inch round baking pans. Sprinkle *each* pan with ¼ cup chopped *pecans.* Place rolls in prepared pans (step 6). Cover; let rise till nearly double (about 30 minutes). Bake in 375° oven 20 to 25 minutes. Invert onto serving plate.

Cinnamon Rolls: Prepare Basic Sweet Roll dough as directed. Divide dough in half. Roll one *half* of dough into a 12x8-inch rectangle. Melt 3 tablespoons *butter or margarine;* spread *half* over dough (step 1). Combine ½ cup granulated *sugar* and 2 teaspoons *ground cinnamon;* sprinkle *half* over dough. If desired, measure ¾ cup *raisins;* sprinkle *about half* over dough. Roll up jelly-roll-style, beginning from longest side (step 2). Seal (step 3). Slice into 12 pieces (step 4). Place in greased 9x1½-inch round baking pan. Repeat with remaining. Cover; let rise till nearly double (about 30 minutes). Bake in 375° oven for 20 to 25 minutes. Cool slightly; remove from pans. If desired, drizzle with Confectioners' Icing.

Confectioners' Icing: Combine 1 cup sifted *powdered sugar,* ¼ teaspoon *vanilla,* and enough *milk* to make of drizzling consistency (about 1½ tablespoons).

1

Prepare Basic Sweet Roll dough as directed at left. On lightly floured surface, roll out *half* of the dough into a 12x8-inch rectangle.

In small saucepan melt 3 tablespoons *butter or margarine*; brush *half* over one rectangle of dough, as shown.

2

Stir together the sugar and cinnamon as directed for each variation. Add chopped walnuts for *Creamy Cinnamon Rolls* variation. Sprinkle *half* of the sugar mixture atop one rectangle of dough. Sprinkle with raisins, if desired, for *Cinnamon Rolls* variation. Roll up jelly-roll-style, beginning from longest end, as shown. (To make fewer larger rolls, roll dough from the shortest side.)

3

Pinch edges of dough together to seal firmly, as shown. Moistening the edges of the dough with water makes them easier to seal firmly.

4

Slice each roll of dough into 12 pieces. Instead of using a sharp knife (which is apt to squash the rolls), use a piece of ordinary sewing-weight or heavy-duty thread. Place thread under rolled dough where you want to make the cut; pull thread up around sides. Crisscross thread across top of roll, pulling quickly as though tying a knot, as shown. Repeat with remaining dough.

5

For *Creamy Cinnamon Rolls*, place rolls in greased pans. Cover; let rise till nearly double (about 30 minutes). Using ¾ cup *whipping cream*, pour *half* over each pan of rolls, as shown. Bake in 375° oven for 20 to 25 minutes. Cool slightly; invert onto serving plate.

6

For *Caramel-Pecan Rolls*, place cut rolls atop pans filled with brown sugar mixture and sprinkled with pecans, as shown. Cover; let rise till nearly double (about 30 minutes). Bake in 375° oven for 20 to 25 minutes. Cool slightly. Invert onto serving plate.

Glazed Orange Rolls (pictured on pages 6 and 7)

4 to 4½ cups all-purpose flour
1 package active dry yeast
1 cup milk
½ cup granulated sugar
3 tablespoons butter *or* margarine
½ teaspoon salt
3 eggs
½ cup granulated sugar
6 tablespoons butter *or*
   margarine, softened
2 teaspoons finely shredded
   orange peel
1½ cups sifted powdered sugar
2 to 3 tablespoons orange juice

In large mixer bowl combine *2 cups* of the flour and the yeast. In saucepan heat milk, ½ cup sugar, 3 tablespoons butter or margarine, and salt just till warm (115° to 120°) and butter is almost melted; stir constantly. Add to flour mixture; add eggs. Beat at low speed of electric mixer for ½ minute, scraping bowl. Beat 3 minutes at high speed. Stir in as much of the remaining flour as you can mix in with a spoon. Turn out onto lightly floured surface. Knead in enough of the remaining flour to make a moderately soft dough that is smooth and elastic (3 to 5 minutes total). Shape into a ball. Place in lightly greased bowl, turning once to grease surface. Cover; let rise in warm place till double (1 to 1½ hours).

Punch down; divide in half. Cover; let rest 10 minutes. Roll *half* into a 12x8-inch rectangle. Combine ½ cup sugar, 6 tablespoons softened butter or margarine, and orange peel; spread *half* of mixture over dough. Roll up jelly-roll-style, beginning with long side; seal seams well. Slice into 12 rolls. Place, cut side down, in greased 2½-inch muffin pans. (Or, use two 8x1½-inch round baking pans for softer rolls.) Repeat with remaining dough and sugar mixture. Cover; let rise till nearly double (about 1¼ hours). Bake in 375° oven for 15 to 20 minutes. Remove from pan immediately. Combine powdered sugar and enough orange juice to make of drizzling consistency. Drizzle over warm rolls. Makes 24 rolls.

Whole Wheat Prune Rolls

1½ cups water
1 cup pitted dried prunes
1½ to 2 cups all-purpose flour
1 package active dry yeast
¾ cup milk
2 tablespoons sugar
2 tablespoons shortening
1 teaspoon salt
1 cup whole wheat flour
2 tablespoons butter *or*
   margarine, melted
3 tablespoons sugar
1 teaspoon ground cinnamon
   Confectioners' Icing (see
   recipe, page 34)

In saucepan combine water and the prunes; cook, covered, about 15 minutes or till tender. Drain, reserving ¼ cup liquid; chop prunes. In large mixer bowl combine *1 cup* of the all-purpose flour and the yeast. In saucepan heat the reserved ¼ cup prune liquid, milk, 2 tablespoons sugar, shortening, and salt just till warm (115° to 120°) and shortening is almost melted; stir constantly. Add milk mixture to flour mixture. Beat at low speed of electric mixer for ½ minute, scraping sides of bowl. Beat 3 minutes at high speed. Stir in whole wheat flour, ½ *cup* of the chopped prunes, and as much of the remaining all-purpose flour as you can mix in with a spoon. Turn out onto lightly floured surface. Knead in enough of the remaining all-purpose flour to make a moderately soft dough that is smooth and elastic (3 to 5 minutes total). Shape into a ball. Place in greased bowl; turn once to grease surface. Cover; let rise in warm place till double (about 1 hour).

Punch down; let rest 10 minutes. Roll into an 18x6-inch rectangle. Brush with the melted butter or margarine. Combine remaining prunes, 3 tablespoons sugar, and cinnamon; spread over dough. Roll up jelly-roll-style, beginning from longest side; seal seams. Cut into 1-inch slices. Place in two greased 8x1½-inch round baking pans. Cover; let rise till nearly double (30 to 45 minutes). Bake in 375° oven for 20 to 25 minutes. Drizzle warm rolls with Confectioners' Icing. Makes 18 rolls.

Kolache

1 **package active dry yeast**
¼ **cup warm water (110° to 115°)**
3¾ **to 4¼ cups all-purpose flour**
¼ **teaspoon ground cinnamon**
¾ **cup milk**
½ **cup butter** *or* **margarine**
¼ **cup granulated sugar**
1 **teaspoon salt**
2 **eggs**
1 **teaspoon finely shredded lemon peel**
  Prune, Apricot, *or* **Poppy Seed Filling**
  Sifted powdered sugar

Soften yeast in water. Combine 2 *cups* flour and the cinnamon. Heat milk, butter, granulated sugar, and salt just till warm (115° to 120°) and butter is almost melted; stir constantly. Add to flour mixture; add yeast, eggs, and lemon peel. Beat at low speed ½ minute. Beat 3 minutes at high speed. Stir in as much of remaining flour as you can mix in with a spoon. On lightly floured surface, knead in enough of remaining flour to make a moderately soft dough that is smooth and elastic (3 to 5 minutes total). Shape into a ball. Place in greased bowl; turn. Cover; let rise in warm place till double (1 to 1½ hours).

Punch down; turn out onto lightly floured surface. Divide dough in half. Cover; let rest 10 minutes. Shape each half into 9 balls; place 3 inches apart on greased baking sheets. Flatten each to a 3-inch circle. Cover; let rise till nearly double (about 45 minutes). Make a depression in center of each; fill with Prune, Apricot, or Poppy Seed Filling. Bake in 375° oven 12 to 15 minutes. Remove from baking sheets; cool. Dust with powdered sugar. Makes 18.

Prune Filling: In saucepan cover 2 cups coarsely snipped *pitted dried prunes* with 1 inch of *water*. Simmer 10 minutes; drain. Stir in ½ cup chopped *nuts*, ⅓ cup granulated *sugar*, 2 teaspoons *lemon juice*, and ½ teaspoon *ground cinnamon*.

Apricot Filling: In saucepan cover 2 cups coarsely snipped *dried apricots* with 1 inch *water*. Simmer 10 minutes; drain. Stir in ⅓ cup granulated *sugar*, 1 tablespoon *butter* or *margarine*, and ½ teaspoon *ground nutmeg*.

Poppy Seed Filling: Cover ¾ cup *poppy seed* (4 ounces) with 1 cup *boiling water*; let stand 30 minutes. Drain thoroughly. Grind poppy seed, using blender or finest blade of food grinder. Stir in ½ cup chopped *nuts*, ⅓ cup *honey*, and 1 teaspoon finely shredded *lemon peel*. Fold in 1 stiff-beaten egg white.

Lemon Candy Canes

1 **package active dry yeast**
½ **cup warm water (110° to 115°)**
2¾ **to 3¼ cups all-purpose flour**
3 **tablespoons granulated sugar**
1 **teaspoon salt**
1 **egg**
⅓ **cup dairy sour cream**
3 **tablespoons butter** *or* **margarine, softened**
½ **cup chopped walnuts**
⅓ **cup granulated sugar**
3 **tablespoons butter** *or* **margarine, melted**
1 **tablespoon finely shredded lemon peel**
1 **cup sifted powdered sugar**
1 **tablespoon lemon juice**
1 **tablespoon water**
¼ **teaspoon vanilla**

Soften yeast in ½ cup water. Combine *1¼ cups* flour, 3 tablespoons granulated sugar, and salt. Add yeast, egg, sour cream, and 3 tablespoons softened butter. Beat at low speed of electric mixer ½ minute. Beat 3 minutes at high speed. Stir in as much of remaining flour as you can mix in with a spoon. On floured surface, knead in enough of remaining flour to make a moderately soft dough that is smooth (3 to 5 minutes total). Shape into a ball in greased bowl; turn. Cover; let rise till double (1 to 1¼ hours). Punch down; divide in half. Cover; let rest 10 minutes.

Combine walnuts, ⅓ cup granulated sugar, 3 tablespoons melted butter, and lemon peel. Roll each *half* of dough into a 12x8-inch rectangle; spread with *half* the nut mixture. Fold in half lengthwise; seal long edges. Cut crosswise into 1-inch strips. Holding both ends, twist each strip. Place on greased baking sheets; curve each folded end to form a cane. Cover; let rise till nearly double (about 30 minutes). Bake in 375° oven 12 to 14 minutes. Blend the powdered sugar and remaining ingredients; frost. Makes 24.

Cinnamon Crisps

3½ to 4 cups all-purpose flour
 1 package active dry yeast
1¼ cups milk
 ¼ cup granulated sugar
 ¼ cup shortening
 1 teaspoon salt
 1 egg
 ½ cup packed brown sugar
 ½ cup granulated sugar
 ¼ cup butter *or* margarine, melted
 ½ teaspoon ground cinnamon
 ¼ cup butter *or* margarine, melted
 1 cup granulated sugar
 ½ cup chopped pecans
 1 teaspoon ground cinnamon

Combine *2 cups* flour and the yeast. Heat milk, ¼ cup granulated sugar, shortening, and salt just till warm (115° to 120°); stir constantly. Add to flour mixture; add egg. Beat at low speed of electric mixer ½ minute. Beat 3 minutes at high speed. Stir in as much of remaining flour as you can mix in with a spoon. On lightly floured surface, knead in enough of remaining flour to make a moderately soft dough that is smooth and elastic (3 to 5 minutes total). Shape into a ball. Place in lightly greased bowl; turn once to grease surface. Cover; let rise till double (1 to 1½ hours).

Punch down; divide in half. Cover; let rest 10 minutes. Roll *half* of dough into a 12-inch square. Combine brown sugar, ½ cup granulated sugar, ¼ cup melted butter, and ½ teaspoon ground cinnamon; spread *half* over dough. Roll up jelly-roll-style, beginning from longest side; seal seams. Cut into 12 rolls. Place on greased baking sheets 3 to 4 inches apart. Flatten each to about 3 inches in diameter. Repeat with remaining dough and sugar mixture. Cover; let rise till nearly double (about 30 minutes). Cover with waxed paper. Use rolling pin to flatten to ⅛-inch thickness; remove paper. Brush rolls with ¼ cup melted butter. Combine 1 cup granulated sugar, pecans, and 1 teaspoon ground cinnamon. Sprinkle over rolls. Cover with waxed paper; roll flat. Remove paper. Bake in 400° oven 10 to 12 minutes. Remove immediately. Makes 24.

Cran-Apple-Filled Rolls

 1 13¾-ounce package hot roll mix
 ¾ cup warm water (110° to 115°)
 ¼ cup sugar
 ½ teaspoon ground nutmeg
 1 beaten egg
 1 cup chopped apple
 ½ cup sugar
 ½ cup fresh *or* frozen cranberries
 ¼ cup chopped walnuts
 1 tablespoon butter *or* margarine
     Confectioners' Icing (see
       recipe, page 34)

Soften yeast from hot roll mix in the warm water. Stir in the flour from hot roll mix, the ¼ cup sugar, nutmeg, and egg; mix well. Cover; refrigerate at least 2 hours. In saucepan cook and stir apple, ½ cup sugar, and cranberries over medium heat 10 minutes or till tender; remove from heat. Stir in walnuts and butter; cool. On lightly floured surface, roll chilled dough into an 18x10-inch rectangle. Cut into eighteen 10-inch strips. Roll each strip into a rope; coil loosely to form round rolls on greased baking sheets. Make a slight indentation in center of each roll; fill *each* with about 1 *tablespoon* apple mixture. Cover; let rise till almost double (30 to 45 minutes). Bake in 375° oven about 15 minutes. Drizzle with Confectioners' Icing. Makes 18.

Easy Peanut Butter Puffs

 1 16-ounce loaf frozen bread
     dough, thawed
 ¼ cup peanut butter
 ¼ cup chopped peanuts
 2 tablespoons honey
 1 teaspoon ground cinnamon

Divide dough into 16 pieces; pat each into a 3-inch circle. Combine peanut butter, peanuts, honey, and cinnamon; place a rounded teaspoonful in center of *each* circle of dough. Wrap dough around mixture to form a ball; pinch edges to seal. Place, seam side down, in greased 9x9x2-inch baking pan. Cover; let rise till almost double (about 1 hour). Bake in 375° oven for 25 to 30 minutes; cover with foil last 10 minutes to prevent overbrowning. Turn out onto wire rack; cool. Makes 16.

Covered with chopped pecans and buttery cinnamon-sugar, *Cinnamon Crisps* are
the homemade version of the bake shop specialty, also known as elephant ears and krispies.

Yeast Doughnuts (pictured on pages 6 and 7)

3 to 3½ cups all-purpose flour
2 packages active dry yeast
¾ cup milk
⅓ cup granulated sugar
¼ cup shortening
1 teaspoon salt
2 eggs
   Shortening *or* cooking oil for
      deep-fat frying
   Confectioners' Icing (see
      recipe, page 34) *or* granulated
      sugar

In mixer bowl combine *1½ cups* flour and the yeast. Heat milk, sugar, ¼ cup shortening, and salt just till warm (115° to 120°) and shortening is almost melted; stir constantly. Add to flour; add eggs. Beat at low speed of electric mixer ½ minute, scraping bowl. Beat 3 minutes at high speed. Stir in as much of remaining flour as you can mix in with a spoon. Turn out onto lightly floured surface. Knead in enough of remaining flour to make a moderately soft dough that is smooth and elastic (3 to 5 minutes total). Shape into a ball. Place in greased bowl; turn once. Cover; let rise in warm place till double (1 to 1¼ hours).

Punch down; turn out onto lightly floured surface. Divide in half. Cover; let rest 10 minutes. Roll each half of dough to ½-inch thickness. Cut with floured doughnut cutter (step 1). Cover; let rise till *very light* (45 to 60 minutes). Heat oil or shortening to 375°. Carefully add 2 or 3 doughnuts; fry about 1 minute (step 2). Turn and fry about 1 minute more (step 3); drain. Glaze with Confectioners' Icing or shake in bag of granulated sugar. Makes 16 to 18 doughnuts.

Orange Yeast Doughnuts: Prepare Yeast Doughnut dough as above, *except* decrease milk to *¼ cup* and add 2 teaspoons finely shredded *orange peel and ½* cup *orange juice* to heated mixture. Continue as directed. For glaze, substitute *orange juice* for the milk in Confectioners' Icing.

Chocolate Yeast Doughnuts: Prepare Yeast Doughnut dough as above, *except* add 2 squares (2 ounces) *semi-sweet chocolate*, cut up, to milk mixture. Heat till chocolate melts; stir constantly. If necessary, cool till just warm (115° to 120°). Continue as directed. For chocolate glaze, combine 1 cup sifted *powdered sugar*; 2 tablespoons *hot water*; 1 square (1 ounce) *semisweet chocolate*, melted; 1 tablespoon *butter or margarine*, melted; and ½ teaspoon *vanilla*. Add some additional water, if necessary, to make of drizzling consistency.

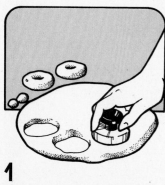

1
On lightly floured surface, roll out each half of dough to ½-inch thickness. Use as little flour as possible to keep dough soft. Cut with floured doughnut cutter, pressing straight down.

2
Fill saucepan ⅓ to ½ full of cooking oil or shortening. Heat to 375°. Gently lower doughnuts into hot fat with metal spatula. Fry only 2 or 3 at a time to prevent fat-soaked doughnuts.

3
After about 1 minute, when doughnut is golden, turn and fry second side about 1 minute more or till golden. Use a two-pronged fork or slotted spoon for easy turning.

Bismarcks

3 to 3½ cups all-purpose flour
2 packages active dry yeast
¾ cup milk
⅓ cup granulated sugar
¼ cup shortening
1 teaspoon salt
2 eggs
　Shortening *or* cooking oil for
　　deep-fat frying
　Chocolate *or* Butterscotch
　　Filling, *or* jelly *or* jam
　Sifted powdered sugar

In large mixer bowl combine *1½ cups* of the flour and the yeast. In saucepan heat together milk, granulated sugar, the ¼ cup shortening, and the salt just till warm (115° to 120°) and shortening is almost melted; stir constantly. Add to flour mixture; add eggs. Beat at low speed of electric mixer for ½ minute, scraping sides of bowl. Beat 3 minutes at high speed. Stir in as much of the remaining flour as you can mix in with a spoon.

Turn out onto lightly floured surface. Knead in enough of the remaining flour to make a moderately soft dough that is smooth and elastic (3 to 5 minutes total). Shape into a ball. Place in lightly greased bowl; turn once to grease surface. Cover; let rise in warm place till almost double (45 to 60 minutes). Roll out, cut, allow to rise, fry, and fill as directed in tip box below. Makes 24.

Chocolate Filling: In small saucepan combine ½ cup *granulated sugar*, 2 tablespoons all-purpose *flour*, and ¼ teaspoon *salt*. Add 1 cup *milk* and 1 square (1 ounce) unsweetened *chocolate*, cut up. Cook and stir over medium heat till thickened and bubbly. Cook and stir 2 minutes more. Gradually stir *half* of the hot mixture into 1 beaten *egg*; return to remaining hot mixture in pan. Cook and stir till just bubbly. Remove from heat. Stir in 1 tablespoon *butter or margarine* and 1 teaspoon *vanilla*. Cover surface with clear plastic wrap. Cool without stirring. Makes 1¼ cups.

Butterscotch Filling: Prepare Chocolate Filling, *except* omit chocolate, substitute an equal amount of packed *brown sugar* for the granulated sugar, and increase the butter or margarine from 1 to *2 tablespoons*.

Making Bismarcks

A doughnut with a filled center instead of a hole is often called a "bismarck." Prepare the dough and let it rise as directed above. When dough has doubled; punch it down and turn out onto lightly floured surface. Divide dough in *half*; let rest 10 minutes. Roll out each half to about ½-inch thickness. Cut with a floured 2½-inch biscuit cutter, pressing straight down. Reroll and cut trimmings.

Cover; let rounds of dough rise in warm place till *very light* (about 30 minutes). Heat oil or shortening to 375°. Fry, 2 or 3 at a time, about 1 minute per side or till golden brown; drain.

Using a sharp knife, cut a wide slit in side of each bismarck. Using a spoon, insert *2 teaspoons* Chocolate or Butterscotch Filling or jelly or jam into *each* bismarck, as shown. Or, fit a decorating bag with a medium writing tube; fill bag with desired filling. Insert tube into slit in each bismarck and squeeze in *about 2 teaspoons* filling. Roll in powdered sugar.

Finnish Braid

5 to 5½ cups all-purpose flour
2 packages active dry yeast
½ teaspoon ground cardamom
1 cup milk
½ cup butter *or* margarine
½ cup sugar
1 teaspoon salt
2 eggs
1 tablespoon finely shredded
orange peel
⅓ cup orange juice
1 egg yolk
1 tablespoon milk

In large mixer bowl combine *2 cups* of the flour, the yeast, and ground cardamom. In saucepan heat the 1 cup milk, the butter or margarine, sugar, and salt just till warm (115° to 120°) and butter is almost melted, stirring constantly. Add to flour mixture in mixer bowl; add the 2 eggs, orange peel, and orange juice.

Beat at low speed of electric mixer for ½ minute, scraping sides of bowl constantly. Beat 3 minutes at high speed. Stir in as much of the remaining flour as you can mix in with a spoon.

Turn out onto lightly floured surface. Knead in enough of the remaining flour to make a moderately stiff dough that is smooth and elastic (6 to 8 minutes total). Shape into a ball. Place in greased bowl; turn to grease surface. Cover; let rise in warm place till double (about 1 hour).

Punch dough down. Divide dough in half. Divide *each* half into thirds; shape each portion into a ball. Cover; let rest 10 minutes. Roll each ball into a 16-inch rope. Line up three ropes, 1 inch apart, on greased baking sheet. Braid loosely, beginning in middle and working toward ends (refer to tip on page 45). Pinch ends together and tuck under. Repeat with remaining dough. Cover; let rise in warm place till almost double (about 30 minutes).

Stir together the 1 egg yolk and the 1 tablespoon milk. Brush braids with egg-yolk mixture. Bake in 350° oven for 25 to 30 minutes or till golden brown. Cover loosely with foil the last 5 to 10 minutes to prevent overbrowning. Makes 2 coffee braids.

German Stollen

4 to 4½ cups all-purpose flour
1 package active dry yeast
¼ teaspoon ground cardamom
1¼ cups milk
½ cup butter *or* margarine
¼ cup granulated sugar
1 teaspoon salt
1 egg
1 cup raisins
¼ cup diced mixed candied fruits
and peels, chopped
¼ cup dried currants
¼ cup chopped blanched almonds
2 tablespoons finely shredded
orange peel
1 tablespoon finely shredded
lemon peel
1 cup sifted powdered sugar
2 tablespoons hot water
½ teaspoon butter *or* margarine

Combine *2 cups* of the flour, the yeast, and cardamom. In saucepan heat milk, the ½ cup butter or margarine, granulated sugar, and salt just till warm (115° to 120°) and butter is almost melted; stir constantly. Add to flour mixture; add egg. Beat at low speed of electric mixer for ½ minute; scrape sides of bowl constantly. Beat 3 minutes at high speed. Stir in as much of the remaining flour as you can mix in with a spoon. Stir in raisins, candied fruits and peels, currants, almonds, orange peel, and lemon peel.

Turn out onto lightly floured surface. Knead in enough of the remaining flour to make a moderately soft dough that is smooth and elastic (3 to 5 minutes total). Shape into a ball. Place in a greased bowl; turn once. Cover; let rise in a warm place till double (about 1¾ hours). Punch down; turn out onto a lightly floured surface. Divide into thirds. Cover; let rest 10 minutes.

Roll *one third* of the dough into a 10x6-inch rectangle. Without stretching, fold the long side over to within 1 inch of the opposite side; seal. Place on greased baking sheet; repeat with remaining dough.

Cover; let rise till almost double (about 1 hour). Bake in 375° oven for 18 to 20 minutes or till golden. Combine the powdered sugar, hot water, and ½ teaspoon butter; brush over warm bread. Makes 3.

Lattice Coffee Cake (pictured on pages 6 and 7)

½ cup milk
1 package active dry yeast
6 tablespoons butter *or* margarine
3 tablespoons sugar
½ teaspoon salt
2 eggs
2 cups all-purpose flour
½ cup cherry, apricot, pineapple, *or* strawberry preserves
¼ cup butter *or* margarine, softened
¼ cup sugar
¼ cup chopped almonds
2 tablespoons all-purpose flour
1 teaspoon water

Heat milk just till warm (110° to 115°). Add to yeast, stirring to dissolve; set aside. In small mixer bowl cream together 6 tablespoons butter, 3 tablespoons sugar, and salt. Add 1 egg and 1 egg yolk (reserve 1 egg white); beat well. By hand, stir the 2 cups flour and yeast-milk mixture alternately into creamed mixture. Do not over-beat. Set aside ½ *cup* of dough; spread the remainder in a well-greased 9x9x2-inch baking pan.

For filling, combine choice of preserves, the ¼ cup softened butter, ¼ cup sugar, and almonds; mix well. Spoon over dough in pan, spreading to edges. For lattice top, stir the 2 tablespoons flour into the reserved ½ cup dough. Roll out on floured surface into a 9x4-inch rectangle. Cut into eight 9x½-inch strips. Weave strips in lattice pattern over filling. Combine the reserved egg white and water; brush over strips. Cover; let rise in warm place till double (about 1 hour). Bake in 375° oven for 25 to 30 minutes. Makes 1.

Sally Lunn

1 cup milk
1 package active dry yeast
6 tablespoons butter *or* margarine
¼ cup sugar
1¼ teaspoons salt
2 eggs
3 cups all-purpose flour

In saucepan heat milk just till warm (110° to 115°). Add to yeast, stirring to dissolve; set aside. In small mixer bowl cream together butter or margarine, sugar, and salt. Add eggs, one at a time, beating well after each addition. By hand, stir the flour and yeast-milk mixture alternately into creamed mixture. Beat till smooth; do not over-beat. Cover; let rise till almost double (about 1 hour). Beat batter down; pour into greased 10-cup Turk's-head mold or fluted tube pan. Let rise till almost double (about 30 minutes). Bake in 350° oven about 40 minutes. Makes 1.

Julekage

4½ to 5 cups all-purpose flour
2 packages active dry yeast
¾ teaspoon ground cardamom
1¼ cups milk
½ cup sugar
½ cup butter *or* margarine
1 teaspoon salt
1 egg
1 cup diced mixed candied fruits and peels, chopped
1 cup light raisins
1 slightly beaten egg yolk
2 tablespoons water
Confectioners' Icing (see recipe, page 34)

In large mixer bowl combine 2½ *cups* flour, the yeast, and cardamom. Heat milk, sugar, butter or margarine, and salt just till warm (115° to 120°) and the butter is almost melted; stir constantly. Add to flour mixture; add egg. Beat at low speed of electric mixer ½ minute. Beat 3 minutes at high speed. Stir in candied fruits, raisins, and as much of the remaining flour as you can mix in with a spoon. Turn out onto lightly floured surface. Knead in enough of the remaining flour to make a moderately stiff dough that is smooth and elastic (6 to 8 minutes total). Shape into a ball. Place in lightly greased bowl; turn once. Cover; let rise in warm place till double (about 1½ hours). Punch down; divide in half. Cover; let rest 10 minutes. Shape into 2 round loaves; place on greased baking sheets. Flatten slightly to 6-inch diameter. Cover; let rise till almost double (45 to 60 minutes). Blend egg yolk and water; brush over loaves. Bake in 350° oven 35 minutes or till done. Remove to rack. Drizzle Confectioners' Icing over loaves. Decorate with almonds and candied cherries, if desired. Slice to serve. Makes 2 round loaves.

Apricot Daisy Ring (pictured on the cover)

3 to 3½ cups all-purpose flour
1 package active dry yeast
¾ cup milk
¼ cup butter *or* margarine
2 tablespoons sugar
1 teaspoon salt
2 eggs
½ cup apricot, cherry, strawberry, *or* peach preserves
2 tablespoons chopped nuts
   Confectioners' Icing (see recipe, page 34)

In large mixer bowl combine *1½ cups* of the flour and the yeast. In saucepan heat together milk, butter or margarine, sugar, and salt just till warm (115° to 120°) and butter or margarine is almost melted; stir constantly. Add to flour mixture; add eggs.

Beat at low speed of electric mixer for ½ minute, scraping sides of bowl constantly. Beat 3 minutes at high speed. Stir in as much of the remaining flour as you can mix in with a spoon.

Turn out onto lightly floured surface. Knead in enough of the remaining flour to make a moderately stiff dough that is smooth and elastic (6 to 8 minutes total). Place in greased bowl; turn once to grease surface. Cover; let rise till double (about 1¼ hours). Punch down; cover and let rest 10 minutes. Transfer to greased baking sheet.

Shape into daisy-style coffee ring, referring to tip below. Let rise till nearly double (about 45 minutes). Bake in 375° oven for 20 to 25 minutes or till golden. Combine choice of preserves and the chopped nuts; spread evenly atop bread. Drizzle with Confectioners' Icing. Makes 1 coffee cake.

Shaping a Daisy Ring

To shape a daisy-style coffee ring, transfer risen dough to a greased baking sheet. Roll dough into a 14-inch circle. Place a beverage tumbler in center of dough.

Make 4 cuts in dough at equal intervals, from outside of circle to tumbler. In the same manner, cut each section into 5 strips, making 20 strips total.

Twist 2 strips together, as shown at bottom, left. Continue around circle, making 10 twists; pinch ends. Remove tumbler.

Remove *one* twist; coil and place in center. Coil remaining twists toward center to form daisy design, as shown at bottom, right. Finish preparing daisy ring according to recipe directions.

Easy Apricot-Date Coffee Cake

1 **16-ounce loaf frozen bread dough, thawed**
¼ **cup apricot preserves**
¼ **cup snipped dates**
Confectioners' Icing (see recipe, page 34)

On floured surface, divide dough in half. Roll one half into a 12x7-inch rectangle. Cut up any large pieces of apricot in preserves; spread *half* the preserves down center third of dough; sprinkle with *half* the dates. Fold long sides over to meet at center of filling; seal. Place, seam side down, on greased baking sheet. Snip into strips on long sides, cutting every 1 inch, almost to center. Turn each strip so cut side is up and filling is exposed. Repeat with remaining. Cover; let rise till nearly double (about 40 minutes). Bake in 350° oven 20 minutes or till golden. Drizzle with Confectioners' Icing. Makes 2.

Cardamom Braid

2¾ **cups all-purpose flour**
1 **package active dry yeast**
1 **teaspoon ground cardamom**
¾ **cup milk**
⅓ **cup sugar**
¼ **cup butter *or* margarine**
½ **teaspoon salt**
1 **egg**
Milk
1 **tablespoon sugar**

In mixer bowl combine ¾ *cup* of the flour, the yeast, and cardamom. Heat ¾ cup milk, ⅓ cup sugar, butter, and salt just till warm (115° to 120°); stir constantly. Add to flour mixture; add egg. Beat at low speed of electric mixer ½ minute. Beat 3 minutes at high speed. Stir in as much remaining flour as you can mix in with a spoon. On lightly floured surface knead in enough remaining flour to make a moderately soft dough that is smooth and elastic (3 to 5 minutes total). Shape into a ball. Place in greased bowl; turn once. Cover; let rise till double (about 1¼ hours).

Punch down; divide into thirds. Cover; let rest 10 minutes. Roll each into a 16-inch-long rope. Braid, referring to tip below. Lightly brush with milk; sprinkle with 1 tablespoon sugar. Cover; let rise till nearly double (about 40 minutes). Bake in 375° oven about 20 minutes. Makes 1.

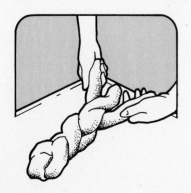

Braiding Dough

Braiding is an easy way to give yeast dough a different look. Simply punch down the risen dough, divide into thirds, and shape into balls; cover. Let rest 10 minutes. Form each ball into a rope of the length specified in the recipe. Line up the three ropes, 1 inch apart, on a greased baking sheet. Braid loosely, beginning in the middle and working toward ends. (Working from the middle is easier and helps avoid stretching the dough, which results in an uneven loaf.) Braid the ropes loosely, as shown, so the dough has room to expand without cracking or losing its shape. Gently straighten on the baking sheet. Pinch ends of ropes together and tuck the sealed portion under the braid. If desired, brush with a little *milk* and lightly sprinkle with *sugar* for a crusty top, *or* brush with a mixture of beaten *egg white* and *water* for a shiny top.

Choose one or more of your favorite jellies to fill the doughnut rings of *Sunburst Coffee Cake.* The center of this pretty coffee cake is filled with the doughnut ''holes.''

Sunburst Coffee Cake

2½ to 3 cups all-purpose flour
1 package active dry yeast
⅔ cup milk
¼ cup sugar
¼ cup shortening
1 teaspoon salt
1 egg
1 teaspoon finely shredded lemon
   peel
¼ cup raspberry, currant, cherry,
   or strawberry jelly
1½ cups sifted powdered sugar
3 tablespoons lemon juice
¼ teaspoon vanilla
¼ cup chopped pecans or toasted
   sliced almonds

In large mixer bowl combine *1 cup* of the flour and the yeast. In saucepan heat milk, sugar, shortening, and salt just till warm (115° to 120°) and shortening is almost melted; stir constantly. Add to flour mixture; stir in egg and lemon peel. Beat at low speed of electric mixer for ½ minute, scraping sides of bowl constantly. Beat 3 minutes at high speed. Stir in as much of the remaining flour as you can mix in with a spoon.

Turn out onto lightly floured surface. Knead in enough of the remaining flour to make a moderately soft dough that is smooth and elastic (3 to 5 minutes total). Shape into a ball. Place in lightly greased bowl; turn once to grease surface. Cover; let rise in warm place till double (1 to 1½ hours).

Punch down. Cover; let rest 10 minutes. Roll out into a 10x8-inch rectangle. With floured doughnut cutter, cut into 12 doughnuts; arrange in a circle on greased baking sheet. Stretch the doughnut rings slightly with fingers to elongate. Cluster "holes" in center, cutting additional "holes" from dough scraps. Let rise till light (about 45 minutes). Bake in 375° oven for 12 to 15 minutes or till golden. Carefully remove from baking sheet. Cool on rack. Spoon choice of jelly into center of doughnut rings. Combine powdered sugar, lemon juice, and vanilla; drizzle over coffee cake. Sprinkle center with chopped pecans or toasted almonds. Makes 1 coffee cake.

Cinnamon Crescents

3½ to 4 cups all-purpose flour
1 package active dry yeast
¾ cup milk
⅓ cup sugar
6 tablespoons butter *or* margarine
½ teaspoon salt
3 eggs
1 cup raisins
½ cup sugar
½ cup chopped walnuts
2 tablespoons butter *or*
   margarine, melted
1 teaspoon ground cinnamon
   Confectioners' Icing (see
   recipe, page 34)
¼ cup chopped walnuts

In large mixer bowl combine *1½ cups* of the flour and the yeast. Heat milk, ⅓ cup sugar, 6 tablespoons butter or margarine, and salt just till warm (115° to 120°) and butter is almost melted; stir constantly. Add to flour mixture; add eggs. Beat at low speed of electric mixer for ½ minute, scraping sides of bowl. Beat 3 minutes at high speed. Stir in as much of the remaining flour as you can mix in with a spoon.

Turn out onto a lightly floured surface. Knead in enough of the remaining flour to make a moderately soft dough that is smooth and elastic (3 to 5 minutes total). Shape into a ball. Place in lightly greased bowl; turn once. Cover; let rise in warm place till double (1 to 1½ hours).

Punch down; divide dough in half. Cover; let rest 10 minutes. Roll *each half* into a 12x10-inch rectangle. Brush with a little water. Combine raisins, the ½ cup sugar, ½ cup chopped nuts, the 2 tablespoons melted butter or margarine, and cinnamon; sprinkle *half* over each rectangle. Roll up starting with long edge; seal seams.

Place, seam side down, on greased baking sheets, curving to form crescent shape; pinch ends to seal. Cover; let rise till nearly double (about 30 minutes). Bake in 350° oven 20 to 25 minutes or till golden. If necessary, cover with foil the last 15 minutes to prevent overbrowning. Drizzle Confectioners' Icing over both coffee cakes; sprinkle each with *half* of the ¼ cup chopped walnuts. Makes 2 coffee cakes.

Sourdough Breads

Sourdough Starter

1 package active dry yeast
2½ cups warm water (110° to 115°)
2 cups all-purpose flour
1 tablespoon sugar *or* honey

Dissolve yeast in ½ *cup* water. Stir in remaining 2 cups water, the flour, and sugar or honey. Beat till smooth. Cover with cheesecloth. Let stand at room temperature for 5 to 10 days or till bubbly; stir 2 to 3 times each day. (Fermentation time depends upon room temperature. A warmer room hastens the fermentation process.)

To store, transfer Sourdough Starter to a jar and cover with cheesecloth; refrigerate. *Do not cover jar tightly with a metal lid.* To use Starter, bring desired amount to room temperature. To replenish Starter after using, stir ¾ cup *all-purpose flour*, ¾ cup *water*, and 1 teaspoon *sugar or honey* into remaining amount. Cover; let stand at room temperature at least 1 day or till bubbly. Refrigerate for later use.

If Starter isn't used within 10 days, stir in 1 teaspoon *sugar or honey*. Repeat every 10 days until used.

Sourdough Pancakes

1 cup Sourdough Starter
1¼ cups all-purpose flour
2 tablespoons sugar
1 teaspoon baking powder
½ teaspoon baking soda
½ teaspoon salt
1 beaten egg
1 cup milk
1 tablespoon cooking oil

Bring Sourdough Starter to room temperature. In mixing bowl combine flour, sugar, baking powder, soda, and salt. Combine egg, milk, oil, and Starter. Add all at once to flour mixture; stir till blended but still slightly lumpy. Pour about ¼ *cup* batter onto hot, lightly greased griddle or heavy skillet for each pancake. Cook till golden, turning to cook other side when pancakes have a bubbly surface and slightly dry edges. Makes about twelve 4-inch pancakes.

Sourdough Buttermilk Pancakes: Prepare Sourdough Pancake batter as above, *except* decrease baking powder to ½ *teaspoon*, substitute 1¼ cups *buttermilk* for the milk, and increase cooking oil to *2 tablespoons*. Batter will be thick; thin with additional buttermilk, if necessary. Pour out batter as above, gently spreading with a spoon.

Sourdough Bread

1 cup Sourdough Starter
1 package active dry yeast
1½ cups warm water (110° to 115°)
5½ to 6 cups all-purpose flour
2 teaspoons salt
2 teaspoons sugar
½ teaspoon baking soda

Bring Sourdough Starter to room temperature. In large bowl dissolve yeast in water. Stir in 2½ *cups* flour, salt, sugar, and Starter. Combine 2½ *cups* flour and soda; stir into sourdough mixture. Stir in as much remaining flour as you can mix in with a spoon. Turn out onto lightly floured surface. Knead in enough remaining flour to make a moderately stiff dough that is smooth and elastic (6 to 8 minutes total). Shape into a ball in greased bowl; turn once. Cover; let rise in warm place till double (1 to 1½ hours).

Punch down; divide in half. Cover; let rest 10 minutes. Shape *each* half into a 6-inch round or 9x4-inch oblong loaf on greased baking sheet. With sharp knife, make crisscross slashes across tops. Cover; let rise till nearly double (about 1 hour). Bake in 400° oven 35 to 40 minutes. Remove from baking sheet; cool on wire rack. Makes 2.

A unique, chewy texture and slightly tangy flavor are the exceptional hallmarks of
Sourdough Bread, Sourdough Pancakes, and *Orange-Cinnamon Sourdough Rolls* (see recipe, page 52).

Sourdough Wheat Bread

1 **cup Sourdough Starter (see recipe, page 48)**
1 **package active dry yeast**
1½ **cups warm water (110° to 115°)**
3 **cups whole wheat flour**
¼ **cup dark molasses**
3 **tablespoons butter *or* margarine, softened**
2 **teaspoons salt**
2½ **to 3 cups all-purpose flour**
½ **teaspoon baking soda**
½ **cup wheat germ**

Bring Sourdough Starter to room temperature. Dissolve yeast in water. Stir in whole wheat flour, molasses, butter, salt, and Starter. Combine *1 cup* of the all-purpose flour and the soda; stir into sourdough mixture. Stir in wheat germ. Stir in as much remaining all-purpose flour as you can mix in with a spoon. On lightly floured surface, knead in enough remaining all-purpose flour to make a moderately stiff dough that is smooth and elastic (6 to 8 minutes total). Shape into a ball. Place in greased bowl; turn once. Cover; let rise in warm place till double (1½ to 2 hours).

Punch down; divide in half. Cover; let rest 10 minutes. Shape into 2 loaves; place in two greased 8x4x2-inch loaf pans. Cover; let rise till nearly double (about 1 hour). Bake in 375° oven for 35 to 40 minutes; cover with foil for last 10 to 15 minutes if bread browns too quickly. Remove from pans; cool on wire racks. Makes 2 loaves.

Sourdough Rye Bread

1 **cup Sourdough Starter (see recipe, page 48)**
1 **package active dry yeast**
1½ **cups warm water (110° to 115°)**
3 **cups rye flour**
¼ **cup sugar**
3 **tablespoons butter *or* margarine, softened**
2 **teaspoons salt**
1 **teaspoon caraway seed**
3 **to 3½ cups all-purpose flour**
½ **teaspoon baking soda**

Bring Sourdough Starter to room temperature. Dissolve yeast in water. Stir in rye flour, sugar, butter, salt, caraway, and Starter. Combine *1 cup* all-purpose flour and the soda; stir into sourdough mixture. Stir in as much remaining all-purpose flour as you can mix in with a spoon. On lightly floured surface, knead in enough remaining all-purpose flour to make a moderately stiff dough that is smooth and elastic (6 to 8 minutes total). Shape into a ball. Place in lightly greased bowl; turn once to grease surface. Cover; let rise in warm place till double (about 1½ hours).

Punch down; divide in half. Cover; let rest 10 minutes. Shape into 2 loaves. Place in greased 8x4x2-inch loaf pans. Cover; let rise till nearly double (about 1 hour). Bake in 375° oven 35 to 40 minutes; cover with foil last 10 to 15 minutes if bread browns too quickly. Cool on rack. Makes 2.

Sourdough Raisin Bread

1½ **cups Sourdough Starter (see recipe, page 48)**
1 **package active dry yeast**
1 **cup warm water (110° to 115°)**
3¾ **to 4¼ cups all-purpose flour**
¼ **cup butter *or* margarine, softened**
2 **tablespoons brown sugar**
1 **teaspoon salt**
½ **teaspoon baking soda**
1½ **cups raisins (8 ounces)**
1 **beaten egg white**
1 **tablespoon granulated sugar**
½ **teaspoon ground cinnamon**

Bring Sourdough Starter to room temperature. Dissolve yeast in water. Stir in 2½ *cups* of the flour, butter, brown sugar, and Starter. Combine ½ *cup* of the flour, the salt, and soda; stir into sourdough mixture. Stir in raisins. Stir in as much remaining flour as you can mix in with a spoon. On lightly floured surface, knead in enough remaining flour to make a moderately stiff dough that is smooth and elastic (6 to 8 minutes total). Shape into a ball. Place in greased bowl; turn once. Cover; let rise in warm place till double (about 1½ hours).

Punch down; divide in half. Cover; let rest 10 minutes. Shape *each* half into a 6-inch round on lightly greased baking sheet. Cover; let rise till nearly double (about 1 hour). Brush loaves with beaten egg white and sprinkle with a mixture of granulated sugar and cinnamon. Bake in 350° oven about 35 minutes or till golden. Cover with foil for last 10 minutes if bread browns too quickly. Cool. Makes 2 loaves.

Sourdough English Muffins

1 cup Sourdough Starter (see
  recipe, page 48)
1 package active dry yeast
¼ cup warm water (110° to 115°)
½ cup buttermilk
2¾ cups all-purpose flour
6 tablespoons yellow cornmeal
1 teaspoon baking soda
1 teaspoon salt

Bring Sourdough Starter to room temperature. Dissolve yeast in water. In mixing bowl stir together Starter and buttermilk; stir in yeast. Combine flour, *4 tablespoons* of the cornmeal, the baking soda, and salt; stir into sourdough mixture. Turn out onto lightly floured surface. Knead till smooth and elastic, 6 to 8 minutes, adding a small amount of additional flour if necessary to prevent sticking. Cover; let rest 10 minutes.

Roll dough to ¼-inch thickness. Using a 4-inch round cutter, cut dough into muffins. Dip in remaining 2 tablespoons cornmeal to coat both sides. Cover; let rise till *very light* (about 45 minutes). Bake on ungreased griddle or in ungreased skillet over medium-low heat for 20 to 30 minutes or till done, turning frequently. Cool on wire rack. Makes 12 muffins.

Sourdough Cheese Rolls

1 cup Sourdough Starter (see
  recipe, page 48)
1 package active dry yeast
¾ cup warm water (110° to 115°)
4 to 4½ cups all-purpose flour
¼ cup sugar
¼ cup butter *or* margarine,
  softened
1 egg
2 teaspoons salt
½ teaspoon baking soda
1 cup shredded cheddar cheese
  (4 ounces)

Bring Sourdough Starter to room temperature. In mixer bowl dissolve yeast in water; mix in *1½ cups* of the flour, the sugar, butter, egg, salt, and Starter. Beat at low speed of electric mixer ½ minute, scraping sides of bowl. Beat 3 minutes at high speed. Combine *1 cup* of the flour and the baking soda; stir into sourdough mixture. Add cheese. Stir in as much remaining flour as you can mix in with a spoon. Turn out onto lightly floured surface. Knead in enough remaining flour to make a moderately stiff dough that is smooth and elastic (6 to 8 minutes total). Shape into a ball. Place in lightly greased bowl; turn once to grease surface. Cover; let rise in warm place till double (about 1½ hours).

Punch down. Cover; let rest 10 minutes. Divide dough into 24 pieces; shape into balls on greased baking sheets. Cover; let rise till nearly double (25 to 30 minutes). Bake in 375° oven about 20 minutes or till golden. Makes 24 rolls.

Sourdough Cornmeal Dinner Rolls

1 cup Sourdough Starter (see
  recipe, page 48)
1 package active dry yeast
¾ cup warm water (110° to 115°)
3¾ to 4¼ cups all-purpose flour
½ cup yellow cornmeal
¼ cup sugar
¼ cup butter *or* margarine,
  softened
1 egg
2 teaspoons salt
½ teaspoon baking soda

Bring Sourdough Starter to room temperature. In mixer bowl dissolve yeast in water. Stir in *1 cup* of the flour, the cornmeal, sugar, butter, egg, salt, and Starter. Beat at low speed of electric mixer ½ minute, scraping sides of bowl. Beat 3 minutes at high speed. Combine *1 cup* flour and the soda; stir into sourdough mixture. Stir in as much remaining flour as you can mix in with a spoon. Turn out onto lightly floured surface. Knead in enough remaining flour to make a moderately stiff dough that is smooth and elastic (6 to 8 minutes total). Shape into a ball. Place in greased bowl; turn once to grease surface. Cover; let rise in warm place till double (about 1½ hours).

Punch down; divide in half. Cover; let rest 10 minutes. Shape into desired rolls, referring to illustrations on page 23. Place 2 to 3 inches apart on greased baking sheets. Cover; let rise till nearly double (about 30 minutes). Bake in 375° oven for 18 to 20 minutes or till golden. Makes 24.

Orange-Cinnamon Sourdough Rolls (pictured on page 49)

¾ cup Sourdough Starter (see recipe, page 48)
2 cups self-rising flour
½ cup buttermilk *or* sour milk
4 tablespoons butter *or* margarine, melted
½ cup sugar
1 tablespoon finely shredded orange peel
2 teaspoons ground cinnamon
Confectioners' Icing (see recipe, page 34)

Bring Sourdough Starter to room temperature. In mixing bowl combine self-rising flour, buttermilk or sour milk, and Sourdough Starter. Turn dough out onto lightly floured surface; knead 15 times. Roll into a 12-inch square. Brush with *3 tablespoons* of the melted butter or margarine. Combine sugar, shredded orange peel, and cinnamon; sprinkle over dough. Roll up, jelly-roll-style, starting from longest side; seal seams. Slice into twelve pieces; place, cut side down, in a greased 9x9x2-inch baking pan. Brush with the remaining 1 tablespoon melted butter or margarine. Bake in 450° oven for 20 to 25 minutes or till golden. Immediately turn out onto wire rack. Drizzle rolls with Confectioners' Icing. Makes 12 rolls.

Sourdough Coffee Cake

⅔ cup Sourdough Starter (see recipe, page 48)
1¼ cups all-purpose flour
½ cup granulated sugar
1½ teaspoons baking powder
¼ teaspoon salt
¼ cup butter *or* margarine
1 beaten egg
1 teaspoon vanilla
1 21-ounce can cherry, blueberry, peach, pineapple, apricot, *or* strawberry pie filling
½ cup all-purpose flour
¼ cup packed brown sugar
½ teaspoon ground cinnamon
¼ cup butter *or* margarine

Bring Sourdough Starter to room temperature. In mixing bowl stir together the 1¼ cups flour, the granulated sugar, baking powder, and salt. Cut in ¼ cup butter or margarine till mixture resembles coarse crumbs. Combine Sourdough Starter, egg, and vanilla. Stir into flour mixture, mixing well. Spread in a greased 11x7x1½-inch baking pan. Spoon choice of pie filling over top. Combine the remaining ½ cup flour, the brown sugar, and cinnamon. Cut in the remaining ¼ cup butter or margarine till the mixture resembles coarse crumbs; sprinkle over pie-filling layer. Bake in 350° oven for 45 to 50 minutes. Makes 10 to 12 servings.

Sourdough Banana Nut Loaf

½ cup Sourdough Starter (see recipe, page 48)
2 cups all-purpose flour
2 teaspoons baking powder
¾ teaspoon salt
½ teaspoon baking soda
½ cup butter, margarine, *or* shortening
¼ cup granulated sugar
¼ cup packed brown sugar
2 eggs
⅔ cup mashed ripe banana (2 medium bananas)
½ cup chopped pecans *or* walnuts

Bring Sourdough Starter to room temperature. Thoroughly stir together flour, baking powder, salt, and baking soda; set aside. In mixer bowl cream butter, margarine, or shortening; granulated sugar; and brown sugar till light and fluffy. Add eggs; beat well. Combine the mashed banana and Sourdough Starter. Add flour mixture and banana mixture alternately to creamed mixture. Beat till smooth after each addition. Fold in chopped nuts. Turn batter into greased 9x5x3-inch loaf pan.

Bake in 350° oven for 50 to 55 minutes or till wooden pick inserted near center comes out clean. Remove from pan and cool on wire rack. Wrap and store overnight before slicing. Makes 1 loaf.

Sourdough Muffins

½ cup Sourdough Starter (see recipe, page 48)
1¾ cups all-purpose flour
¼ cup sugar
2½ teaspoons baking powder
1 beaten egg
½ cup milk
⅓ cup cooking oil

Bring Sourdough Starter to room temperature. In large mixing bowl stir together the flour, sugar, baking powder, and ¾ teaspoon *salt*. Make a well in the center. Combine egg, milk, oil, and Sourdough Starter. Add all at once to flour mixture. Stir just till moistened (batter should be lumpy). Spoon into greased or paper-bake-cup-lined muffin cups, filling each about ⅔ full.

Bake in 400° oven for 20 to 25 minutes. Remove from pan; serve warm. Makes 10 to 12 muffins.

Sourdough Honey-Wheat Muffins

½ cup Sourdough Starter (see recipe, page 48)
1 cup all-purpose flour
½ cup whole wheat flour
1 teaspoon baking powder
1 beaten egg
¼ cup honey
¼ cup cooking oil
¼ cup milk
½ teaspoon grated lemon peel

Bring Sourdough Starter to room temperature. In large mixing bowl stir together the all-purpose flour, whole wheat flour, baking powder, and ½ teaspoon *salt*. Make a well in the center. Combine egg, honey, oil, milk, lemon peel, and Sourdough Starter. Add all at once to flour mixture. Stir just till moistened (batter should be lumpy). Spoon into greased muffin cups, filling each about ⅔ full. Bake in 400° oven for 20 to 25 minutes. Remove from pan; serve warm. Makes about 10 muffins.

Sourdough Pumpkin Muffins

½ cup Sourdough Starter (see recipe, page 48)
2 cups all-purpose flour
2 teaspoons baking powder
½ teaspoon baking soda
½ teaspoon ground cinnamon
½ teaspoon ground nutmeg
1 beaten egg
½ cup canned pumpkin
¼ cup milk
¼ cup honey
¼ cup cooking oil

Bring Sourdough Starter to room temperature. In large mixing bowl stir together flour, baking powder, baking soda, cinnamon, nutmeg, and ½ teaspoon *salt*. Make a well in the center. Combine egg, pumpkin, milk, honey, oil, and Sourdough Starter. Add all at once to flour mixture. Stir just till moistened (batter should be lumpy). Spoon into greased muffin cups, filling each about ⅔ full. Bake in 400° oven about 20 minutes. Remove from pan; serve warm. Makes 12 muffins.

Sourdough Cinnamon Drop Biscuits

½ cup Sourdough Starter (see recipe, page 48)
1 cup all-purpose flour
1 tablespoon brown sugar
2 teaspoons baking powder
½ teaspoon ground cinnamon
¼ teaspoon cream of tartar
¼ teaspoon baking soda
¼ teaspoon ground nutmeg
¼ cup shortening
¼ cup milk

Bring Sourdough Starter to room temperature. In mixing bowl stir together the flour, brown sugar, baking powder, cinnamon, cream of tartar, baking soda, nutmeg, and ¼ teaspoon *salt*. Cut in shortening till mixture resembles coarse crumbs. Make a well in the center. Combine Sourdough Starter and milk; add all at once to dry mixture. Stir just till dough clings together.

Use a knife or narrow spatula to push dough from tablespoon onto lightly greased baking sheet. Bake in 425° oven for 12 to 15 minutes or till golden. Serve immediately. Makes 10 to 12 biscuits.

2 QUICK BREADS

This selection of home-baked quick breads includes (clockwise from back left) *Biscuit Bubble Ring, Corn Sticks, Popovers, Eggnog-Cherry Nut Loaf, Easy Lemon-Blueberry Muffins,* and *Fruit-Filled Ladder Loaf.* (See Index for recipe pages.)

Loaves

Banana Nut Bread

1¾ **cups all-purpose flour**
1¼ **teaspoons baking powder**
¾ **teaspoon salt**
½ **teaspoon baking soda**
⅔ **cup sugar**
⅓ **cup shortening**
2 **eggs**
2 **tablespoons milk**
1 **cup mashed ripe banana**
¼ **cup chopped pecans** *or*
   walnuts

In mixing bowl stir together flour, baking powder, salt, and baking soda; set aside.

In mixer bowl cream sugar and shortening with electric mixer till light, scraping sides of bowl often (step 1). Add eggs, one at a time, and the milk, beating till smooth and fluffy after each addition (step 2). Add flour mixture and mashed banana alternately to creamed mixture, beating till smooth after each addition (steps 3, 4, and 5). Gently fold in the chopped pecans or walnuts.

Turn batter into lightly greased 8x4x2-inch loaf pan (step 6). Bake in 350° oven for 60 to 65 minutes or till wooden pick inserted near center comes out clean. Cool in pan 10 minutes. Remove from pan; cool thoroughly on wire rack. For easier slicing, wrap in foil and store overnight. Makes 1 loaf.

1

In mixer bowl beat the shortening and sugar at high speed of electric mixer about 5 minutes or till light, as shown. Scrape sides of bowl often.

Shortening and sugar are creamed together to incorporate air into the mixture, giving the loaf a lighter, more cake-like texture.

2

Add eggs, one at a time, and milk. Beat at medium speed of electric mixer about one minute or till smooth and fluffy after each addition, as shown. Scrape sides of bowl often with a rubber spatula to combine all ingredients.

3

To add flour mixture and mashed banana alternately to the creamed mixture, begin by spooning about ⅓ of the flour mixture over the creamed mixture in mixer bowl.

Beat at low speed of electric mixer just till smooth. Scrape sides of bowl often with a rubber spatula.

4

Add ½ of the mashed banana to the creamed mixture. Beat at low speed just till smooth. Scrape sides of bowl often.

Add another ⅓ of the flour mixture; beat till smooth. Add remaining mashed banana, then remaining flour mixture in the same manner.

5

Mixture should appear smooth and fluffy after beating in all of the flour mixture and banana.

These ingredients are added alternately to help maintain the fluffy quality of the shortening-egg mixture in step 2. Adding one or the other all at once tends to reduce the fluffiness of the batter.

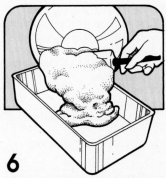

6

Turn the batter into the lightly greased 8x4x2-inch loaf pan, scraping sides of the bowl with a rubber spatula. Lightly spread the batter evenly in the pan.

Eggnog-Cherry Nut Loaf (pictured on pages 54 and 55)

2½ cups all-purpose flour
¾ cup sugar
1 tablespoon baking powder
1 beaten egg
Homemade Eggnog *or* 1¼ cups dairy eggnog
⅓ cup cooking oil
½ cup chopped walnuts *or* pecans
½ cup chopped maraschino cherries

In mixing bowl stir together flour, sugar, baking powder, and 1 teaspoon *salt*. Mix egg, Homemade Eggnog or dairy eggnog, and cooking oil. Stir into dry ingredients, mixing well. Fold in chopped nuts and cherries. Turn into two greased 8x4x2-inch loaf pans. Bake in 350° oven for 45 to 50 minutes or till done. Cool in pans 10 minutes. Remove from pans; cool on wire rack. Makes 2 loaves.

Homemade Eggnog: Beat together 2 *eggs*, 1 cup *light cream*, ¼ cup *sugar*, and ¼ teaspoon *ground nutmeg*. Makes 1¼ cups.

Three-C Bread

2½ cups all-purpose flour
1 cup sugar
1 teaspoon baking powder
1 teaspoon baking soda
½ teaspoon ground mace
3 beaten eggs
½ cup cooking oil
½ cup milk
2 cups shredded carrots
1⅓ cups flaked coconut
½ cup chopped maraschino cherries

In mixing bowl stir together flour, sugar, baking powder, baking soda, mace, and ½ teaspoon *salt*. Combine eggs, oil, and milk. Add to dry ingredients; mix well. Stir in shredded carrots, flaked coconut, and chopped cherries. Pour into three greased 21-ounce pie filling cans. Bake in 350° oven for 1 to 1¼ hours. (Or, pour batter into one greased 9x5x3-inch loaf pan. Bake in 350° oven 45 to 50 minutes.) Cool in cans 10 minutes. Remove from cans; cool completely on wire rack. Wrap and store overnight before slicing. Makes 3 loaves.

Zucchini Nut Loaf

1½ **cups all-purpose flour**
  1 **teaspoon ground cinnamon**
  ½ **teaspoon baking soda**
  ½ **teaspoon ground nutmeg**
  ¼ **teaspoon baking powder**
  1 **cup sugar**
  1 **cup finely shredded unpeeled**
       zucchini
  1 **egg**
  ¼ **cup cooking oil**
  ¼ **teaspoon finely shredded lemon**
       peel
  ½ **cup chopped walnuts**

In mixing bowl stir together flour, cinnamon, baking soda, nutmeg, baking powder, and ½ teaspoon *salt*; set aside. In another mixing bowl beat together sugar, shredded zucchini, and egg. Add oil and lemon peel; mix well. Stir flour mixture into zucchini mixture. Gently fold in chopped nuts. Turn batter into a greased 8x4x2-inch loaf pan. Bake in 350° oven for 55 to 60 minutes or till wooden pick inserted near center comes out clean. Cool in pan 10 minutes. Remove from pan; cool thoroughly on rack. Wrap and store loaf overnight before slicing. Makes 1 loaf.

Sour Cream-Cinnamon Loaves

  2 **cups all-purpose flour**
1½ **teaspoons baking powder**
  1 **teaspoon baking soda**
  ½ **teaspoon salt**
  1 **cup sugar**
  ½ **cup shortening**
  2 **eggs**
  1 **teaspoon vanilla**
  1 **cup dairy sour cream**
  ¼ **cup milk**
  ¼ **cup sugar**
  2 **teaspoons ground cinnamon**
1½ **teaspoons finely shredded**
       orange peel

In mixing bowl stir together flour, baking powder, baking soda, and salt; set aside. In large mixer bowl cream together the 1 cup sugar and shortening till light and fluffy. Add eggs and vanilla; beat well. Blend in sour cream and milk. Add flour mixture to sour cream mixture; mix well. Spread ¼ *of the batter* in *each* of two greased 7½x3½x2-inch loaf pans. Combine the ¼ cup sugar, the cinnamon, and shredded orange peel. Sprinkle all but *1 tablespoon* sugar-cinnamon mixture over the batter in pans. Top each with *half* of the remaining batter. Cut through batter gently with knife to make swirling effect with cinnamon. Sprinkle with remaining sugar-cinnamon mixture. Bake in 350° oven for 35 to 40 minutes. Cool in pans 10 minutes. Remove from pans; cool thoroughly on wire racks. Makes 2 small loaves.

Cranberry-Orange Bread

  3 **medium oranges**
  1 **beaten egg**
  2 **tablespoons cooking oil**
  2 **cups all-purpose flour**
  ¾ **cup granulated sugar**
1½ **teaspoons baking powder**
  1 **teaspoon salt**
  ½ **teaspoon baking soda**
  1 **cup coarsely chopped fresh *or***
       frozen cranberries
  ½ **cup chopped walnuts**
  1 **cup sifted powdered sugar**

Finely shred peel from 1 orange; reserve peel. Squeeze juice from all oranges. Measure ¾ cup juice; reserve remaining juice.

Combine the ¾ cup juice, *1 teaspoon* of the peel, egg, and oil. Stir together flour, granulated sugar, baking powder, salt, and baking soda. Add orange juice mixture; stir just till moistened. Fold in cranberries and walnuts. Turn into one lightly greased 8x4x2-inch loaf pan *or* three 6x3x2-inch loaf pans. Bake in 350° oven 50 to 60 minutes for large pan (30 to 40 minutes for smaller pans) or till wooden pick inserted near center comes out clean. Cool 10 minutes in pan; remove from pan. Cool completely on wire rack. For glaze, blend 1 tablespoon of the reserved orange juice with powdered sugar. Add more juice to make of drizzling consistency. Drizzle atop cooled loaves; garnish with reserved shredded orange peel. Makes 1 large or 3 small loaves.

Apricot-Orange Bread: Prepare Cranberry-Orange Bread as above, *except* substitute 1 cup snipped *dried apricots* for the cranberries. Pour boiling water over apricots; let stand about 5 minutes. Drain well before folding into batter.

Whole Wheat Raisin Bread

    3 cups all-purpose flour
    1 cup whole wheat flour
    2 teaspoons baking powder
 1½ teaspoons baking soda
    1 teaspoon salt
  ½ cup butter *or* margarine
 1½ cups raisins
    1 tablespoon caraway seed
    2 eggs
 1½ cups buttermilk *or* sour milk

Stir together all-purpose flour, whole wheat flour, baking powder, baking soda, and salt. Cut in butter or margarine till mixture is crumbly; stir in raisins and caraway seed.

In small bowl beat eggs. Reserve *1 tablespoon* of the beaten eggs; set aside. Combine remaining beaten eggs and buttermilk or sour milk; add to flour mixture, stirring just till moistened.

Knead gently on lightly floured surface for 10 to 12 strokes. Shape dough into a smooth ball; place in greased 2-quart casserole. With sharp knife, cut a 4-inch cross, ¼ inch deep, across center of loaf. Brush with reserved 1 tablespoon beaten egg.

Bake in 350° oven for 70 to 80 minutes or till wooden pick inserted near center comes out clean. Remove from casserole. Cool thoroughly on wire rack. Slice very thin. Makes 1 loaf.

Pumpkin Nut Bread

    2 cups all-purpose flour
    2 teaspoons baking powder
  ½ teaspoon salt
  ½ teaspoon ground ginger
  ¼ teaspoon baking soda
  ¼ teaspoon ground cloves
    1 cup packed brown sugar
  ⅓ cup shortening
    2 eggs
    1 cup canned pumpkin
  ¼ cup milk
  ½ cup coarsely chopped walnuts
  ½ cup raisins (optional)

In mixing bowl stir together flour, baking powder, salt, ginger, baking soda, and cloves; set aside. In large mixer bowl cream together brown sugar and shortening till light; beat in eggs. Add pumpkin and milk; mix well. Add flour mixture to sugar-pumpkin mixture, mixing well. Stir in chopped nuts and the raisins, if desired.

Turn batter into greased 9x5x3-inch loaf pan. Bake in 350° oven for 55 to 60 minutes or till wooden pick inserted near center comes out clean. Cool in pan 10 minutes. Remove from pan; cool thoroughly on wire rack. Wrap and store overnight before slicing. Makes 1 loaf.

Orange-Bran Bread

    1 cup whole bran cereal
    1 cup orange juice
  ½ cup honey
  ¼ cup sugar
    2 tablespoons shortening
    1 egg
    1 tablespoon finely shredded
      orange peel
 2¼ cups all-purpose flour
 2½ teaspoons baking powder
  ½ teaspoon salt
  ½ teaspoon baking soda

In small mixing bowl combine bran cereal and ½ cup of the orange juice; let stand several minutes.

In another mixing bowl stir together honey, sugar, and shortening. Add egg and shredded orange peel; mix well. Stir together flour, baking powder, salt, and baking soda; add to honey mixture alternately with the remaining orange juice, beating after each addition. Stir in bran-orange juice mixture.

Turn batter into two greased 7½x3½x2-inch loaf pans *or* one 9x5x3-inch loaf pan. Bake in 325° oven for 45 to 50 minutes for small pans (55 to 60 minutes for large pan) or till wooden pick inserted near center comes out clean. Cool loaves in pans for 10 minutes. Remove from pans; cool thoroughly on wire racks. Makes 2 small loaves or 1 large loaf.

Lemon Bread

1¾ **cups all-purpose flour**
 ¾ **cup sugar**
 2 **teaspoons baking powder**
 2 **teaspoons finely shredded
   lemon peel**
 1 **egg**
 ¾ **cup milk**
 ¼ **cup cooking oil**
 1 **tablespoon lemon juice**

In mixing bowl stir together flour, sugar, baking powder, lemon peel, and ½ teaspoon *salt*; set aside. In another mixing bowl beat together egg, milk, cooking oil, and lemon juice. Add flour mixture to egg-lemon mixture, stirring just till moistened. Turn batter into two greased 6x3x2-inch loaf pans. Bake in 350° oven for 40 to 45 minutes or till done. Cool in pans 10 minutes. Remove from pans; cool thoroughly on wire rack. Wrap and store overnight. Makes 2 small loaves.

Boston Brown Bread

 ½ **cup whole wheat flour**
 ¼ **cup all-purpose flour**
 ¼ **cup yellow cornmeal**
 ½ **teaspoon baking powder**
 ¼ **teaspoon baking soda**
 1 **beaten egg**
 ¼ **cup light molasses**
 2 **tablespoons sugar**
 2 **teaspoons cooking oil**
 ¾ **cup buttermilk *or* sour milk**
 ¼ **cup raisins**

Stir together flours, cornmeal, baking powder, soda, and ¼ teaspoon *salt*. In mixing bowl combine egg, molasses, sugar, and oil. Add flour mixture and buttermilk or sour milk alternately to molasses mixture; beat well. Stir in raisins. Turn batter into two well-greased 16-ounce vegetable cans. Cover cans tightly with foil. Place cans on a rack set in large Dutch oven. Pour hot water into Dutch oven to depth of 1 inch. Bring to boiling; reduce heat. Cover; simmer 2½ to 3 hours or till done. Add boiling water as needed. Remove cans from pan; let stand 10 minutes. Remove bread from cans. Serve warm. Makes 2 loaves.

Cherry-Pecan Bread

 2 **cups all-purpose flour**
 1 **teaspoon baking soda**
 ¾ **cup sugar**
 ½ **cup butter *or* margarine**
 2 **eggs**
 1 **teaspoon vanilla**
 1 **cup buttermilk *or* sour milk**
 1 **cup chopped pecans**
 1 **cup chopped maraschino
   cherries**

In bowl thoroughly stir together flour, soda, and ½ teaspoon *salt*; set aside. In large mixer bowl cream together sugar, butter, eggs, and vanilla till light and fluffy. Add flour mixture and buttermilk alternately to creamed mixture. Beat just till blended after each addition. Fold in nuts and cherries. Turn batter into lightly greased 9x5x3-inch loaf pan. Bake in 350° oven 55 to 60 minutes. Cool in pan 10 minutes. Remove from pan; cool. If desired, glaze with Confectioners' Icing (see recipe, page 34). Makes 1.

Applesauce-Fig Loaf

 2 **cups all-purpose flour**
 1 **teaspoon baking powder**
 1 **teaspoon baking soda**
 1 **teaspoon ground cinnamon** .
 ½ **teaspoon ground nutmeg**
 ⅔ **cup sugar**
 ½ **cup butter *or* margarine**
 1 **egg**
 1 **teaspoon vanilla**
 1 **cup applesauce**
 ¼ **cup milk**
 1 **cup finely snipped figs**
 ½ **cup chopped walnuts**

In mixing bowl stir together flour, baking powder, baking soda, cinnamon, and nutmeg; set aside. In large mixer bowl cream sugar and butter or margarine till fluffy. Add egg and vanilla; beat well. Combine applesauce and milk. Add flour mixture and applesauce mixture alternately to creamed mixture; beat well after each addition. Stir in figs and nuts. Turn into greased 9x5x3-inch loaf pan. Bake in 350° oven for 45 to 50 minutes or till done. Let cool in pan 10 minutes. Remove from pan and cool completely on wire rack. Wrap and store overnight. Makes 1 loaf.

Blueberry-Walnut Bread

- 1 cup fresh *or* frozen blueberries
- 1¾ cups all-purpose flour
- ⅔ cup sugar
- 1½ teaspoons baking powder
- ½ teaspoon salt
- ½ teaspoon baking soda
- 1 orange
- 2 tablespoons butter *or* margarine
  Boiling water
- 1 beaten egg
- 1 cup chopped walnuts
- ¼ cup all-purpose flour

Thaw blueberries, if frozen; drain. In mixing bowl stir together the 1¾ cups flour, the sugar, baking powder, salt, and baking soda. Finely shred peel from orange to measure 2 teaspoons. Squeeze juice from orange into measuring cup. Add butter or margarine and enough boiling water to measure ¾ cup liquid. Add to flour mixture in bowl; add beaten egg and orange peel. Stir just till dry ingredients are moistened.

In small bowl toss together blueberries, chopped nuts, and the ¼ cup flour. Carefully stir into batter. Turn batter into greased 8x4x2-inch loaf pan. Bake in 350°oven for 55 to 60 minutes or till wooden pick inserted near center comes out clean. Cool in pan 10 minutes. Remove from pan; cool thoroughly on wire rack. Wrap and store overnight. Makes 1 loaf.

Date-Apple Coffee Bread

- 1 tablespoon instant coffee crystals
- 1 cup boiling water
- 1⅓ cups snipped pitted dates (8 ounces)
- 2¼ cups all-purpose flour
- ¾ cup packed brown sugar
- 2 teaspoons baking powder
- ½ teaspoon salt
- ½ teaspoon baking soda
- 1 beaten egg
- 2 medium apples, peeled, cored, and shredded (1 cup)
- ½ cup chopped walnuts
- 2 tablespoons butter *or* margarine, melted

Dissolve coffee crystals in boiling water; pour over dates. Set aside. In large mixing bowl stir together flour, brown sugar, baking powder, salt, and baking soda. Combine egg, shredded apple, walnuts, melted butter or margarine, and coffee-date mixture. Add to flour mixture, stirring just till moistened. Turn into greased 9x5x3-inch loaf pan. Bake in 350° oven for 60 to 65 minutes or till wooden pick inserted near center comes out clean. Cool in pan 10 minutes. Remove from pan; cool thoroughly on wire rack. Makes 1 loaf.

Honey-Date Nut Bread

- ¾ cup boiling water
- 1 cup pitted whole dates, chopped
- 1 egg
- 1 cup honey
- 1 tablespoon butter *or* margarine, softened
- 1 teaspoon vanilla
- 2 cups all-purpose flour
- 1 teaspoon baking soda
- ½ teaspoon salt
- 1 cup chopped walnuts

In small bowl pour boiling water over dates; let stand till cool. *Do not drain.* In small mixer bowl beat egg at high speed of electric mixer for 2 minutes or till thick and lemon-colored; beat in honey, softened butter or margarine, and vanilla. Stir in undrained dates. Stir together flour, baking soda, and salt. Stir flour mixture and nuts into egg-honey mixture just till moistened.

Turn batter into two greased 7½x3½x2-inch loaf pans *or* one greased 9x5x3-inch loaf pan. Bake in 350° oven for 50 minutes for small pans (65 minutes for large pan) or till wooden pick inserted near center comes out clean. Cool in pans 10 minutes. Remove from pans; cool completely on wire rack. If desired, wrap and store overnight before slicing. Makes 2 small loaves or 1 large loaf.

Doughnuts and Fritters

Cake Doughnuts (pictured on page 65)

3¼ cups all-purpose flour
 2 teaspoons baking powder
 ½ teaspoon salt
 ½ teaspoon ground cinnamon
 ¼ teaspoon ground nutmeg
 2 beaten eggs
 ⅔ cup granulated sugar
 1 teaspoon vanilla
 ⅔ cup milk
 ¼ cup butter *or* margarine, melted
   Shortening *or* cooking oil for
   deep-fat frying
 ½ cup granulated sugar (optional)
 ½ teaspoon ground cinnamon
   (optional)
   Confectioners' Icing (see
   recipe, page 34), Chocolate
   Glaze, *or* Orange Glaze
   (optional)

Stir together first 5 ingredients. In large mixer bowl combine eggs, ⅔ cup sugar, and vanilla; beat till thick. Combine milk and butter. Add flour mixture and milk mixture alternately to egg mixture; beat just till blended after each addition. Cover; chill about 2 hours.

On lightly floured surface, roll dough to ½-inch thickness. Cut with floured 2½-inch doughnut cutter (step 1). Fry in deep, hot fat (375°) about 1 minute per side or till golden, turning once with slotted spoon (step 2). Drain on paper toweling (step 3). While warm, shake in mixture of ½ cup sugar and ½ teaspoon ground cinnamon, if desired. Or, cool and drizzle with Confectioners' Icing, Chocolate Glaze, or Orange Glaze, if desired. Makes 16.

Chocolate Glaze: Melt 1½ squares (1½ ounces) *unsweetened chocolate* and 2 tablespoons *butter*; cool. Stir in 1½ cups sifted *powdered sugar* and 1 teaspoon *vanilla*. Add enough *boiling water* to make of drizzling consistency.

Orange Glaze: Combine 2 cups sifted *powdered sugar*, 1 teaspoon finely shredded *orange peel*, and 2 to 3 tablespoons *orange juice*.

Chocolate Cake Doughnuts: Prepare Cake Doughnut dough as above, *except* omit spices, increase sugar to *1 cup*, and add 1 square (1 ounce) melted and cooled *unsweetened chocolate* with the milk and butter. Roll dough and fry as directed. Drizzle with *Chocolate Glaze*.

1

On lightly floured surface, roll chilled doughnut dough to ½-inch thickness. Cut dough with floured doughnut cutter. Push cutter straight down through dough without twisting. Dip the cutter in flour between cuts. Allow doughnuts to stand for a few minutes before frying so that a delicate, thin crust will form. This thin crust retards the immediate absorption of fat.

2

Use a thermometer specially made for deep-fat frying. The temperature of the fat should be 375°. If the fat temperature is too low, the doughnuts will become fat-soaked; if the fat is too hot, the doughnuts will cook too fast on the outside, leaving an uncooked center. Fry doughnuts, a few at a time, 1 minute per side or till golden. Turn with a slotted spoon.

3

Remove doughnuts from the hot fat with a slotted spoon or fork. Place the doughnuts on a rack covered with paper toweling to drain. While warm, shake doughnuts in a mixture of sugar and cinnamon. Or, glaze with Confectioners' Icing, Chocolate Glaze, or Orange Glaze.

Buttermilk Doughnuts

3¼ cups all-purpose flour
 1 teaspoon baking soda
 ½ teaspoon baking powder
 ½ teaspoon ground nutmeg
 ⅛ teaspoon salt
 2 slightly beaten eggs
 ½ cup sugar
 2 tablespoons butter *or*
   margarine, melted
 1 cup buttermilk
   Shortening *or* cooking oil for
   deep-fat frying

In mixing bowl stir together flour, baking soda, baking powder, nutmeg, and salt; set aside. In large mixer bowl beat eggs and sugar till thick and lemon-colored. Stir in melted butter or margarine. Add flour mixture and buttermilk alternately to egg mixture; beat just till blended after each addition. Cover; chill dough about 2 hours.

Turn dough out onto lightly floured surface. Roll to ½-inch thickness; cut with 2½-inch doughnut cutter. Fry in deep, hot fat (375°) about 1 minute per side or till golden, turning once. Drain on paper toweling. While warm, sprinkle with additional sugar, if desired. Makes 18.

Cocoa-Spice Doughnuts

 4 cups all-purpose flour
 ⅓ cup unsweetened cocoa powder
 4 teaspoons baking powder
 1 teaspoon ground cinnamon
 ¾ teaspoon salt
 ¼ teaspoon baking soda
 2 beaten eggs
1¼ cups granulated sugar
 ¼ cup cooking oil
 1 teaspoon vanilla
 ¾ cup buttermilk *or* sour milk
   Shortening *or* cooking oil for
   deep-fat frying
   Cinnamon Glaze

In mixing bowl stir together the flour, cocoa powder, baking powder, cinnamon, salt, and soda; set aside.

In large mixer bowl beat eggs and granulated sugar about 4 minutes or till thick and lemon-colored. Stir in the ¼ cup cooking oil and vanilla. Add flour mixture and buttermilk alternately to egg mixture. Beat just till blended after each addition. Chill dough about 2 hours. On lightly floured surface, roll dough, half at a time, to ½-inch thickness (keep remaining dough chilled). Cut with floured 2½-inch doughnut cutter.

Fry in deep, hot fat (375°) about 1½ minutes per side or till deep brown; drain on paper toweling. Dip warm doughnuts in Cinnamon Glaze. Makes 24 doughnuts.

Cinnamon Glaze: In small bowl combine 4 cups sifted *powdered sugar*, 1 teaspoon *vanilla*, and ½ teaspoon *ground cinnamon*. Add enough *milk* to make of drizzling consistency.

Spiced Maple Doughnuts

 3 cups all-purpose flour
 2 teaspoons baking powder
 1 teaspoon salt
 ½ teaspoon baking soda
 ½ teaspoon ground nutmeg
 ¼ teaspoon ground cinnamon
 ¼ teaspoon ground ginger
 2 eggs
 ½ cup granulated sugar
 ½ cup maple-flavored syrup
 ⅓ cup buttermilk *or* sour milk
 ¼ cup butter *or* margarine, melted
   Shortening *or* cooking oil for
   deep-fat frying
   Sifted powdered sugar

In mixing bowl stir together flour, baking powder, salt, baking soda, nutmeg, cinnamon, and ginger; set aside. In large mixer bowl beat together eggs, granulated sugar, and maple-flavored syrup till thick. Stir in buttermilk or sour milk and melted butter or margarine. Add flour mixture to egg mixture, stirring just till blended. Cover; chill dough about 2 hours.

Turn dough out onto lightly floured surface. Roll to ½-inch thickness. Cut with floured 2½-inch doughnut cutter. Fry, a few at a time, in deep, hot fat (375°) about 1 minute per side or till golden brown, turning once. Drain on paper toweling. Cool. Dust with powdered sugar. Makes 18 to 20 doughnuts.

Apple Fritter Rings

4 **large tart apples**
1 **cup all-purpose flour**
2 **tablespoons sugar**
1 **teaspoon baking powder**
  Dash salt
1 **beaten egg**
⅔ **cup milk**
1 **teaspoon cooking oil**
  Shortening *or* cooking oil for
    deep-fat frying
¼ **cup sugar**
½ **teaspoon ground cinnamon**

Core and peel apples; cut into ½-inch-thick rings and set aside. In mixing bowl thoroughly stir together flour, the 2 tablespoons sugar, baking powder, and salt. Combine egg, milk, and 1 teaspoon cooking oil; add all at once to flour mixture, stirring just till blended.

In skillet that is at least 2 inches deep, heat 1 inch shortening or cooking oil to 375°. Dip apple slices in batter one at a time. Fry fritters in hot fat about 1½ minutes per side or till golden brown, turning once. Drain on paper toweling. Sprinkle hot fritters with a mixture of the ¼ cup sugar and cinnamon. Serve hot. Makes 16 fritters.

Crullers

1¾ **cups all-purpose flour**
½ **teaspoon salt**
½ **teaspoon ground nutmeg**
¼ **teaspoon ground mace**
⅓ **cup granulated sugar**
¼ **cup butter *or* margarine**
2 **eggs**
2 **tablespoons milk**
  Shortening *or* cooking oil for
    deep-fat frying
  Sifted powdered sugar

In bowl stir together flour, salt, nutmeg, and mace; set aside. In mixer bowl cream together granulated sugar and butter or margarine till light and fluffy. Add eggs, one at a time; beat well after each addition. Beat in milk (batter may appear slightly curdled). By hand, stir in the flour mixture. Cover and chill at least 1 hour.

On lightly floured surface, roll *half* the dough (rolling in one direction only so that doughnuts will puff) into a 16x8-inch rectangle. Cut into 2-inch squares (do not reroll). (If desired, use pastry wheel for decorative edges.) Repeat with remaining dough. Fry in deep, hot fat (375°) about 45 seconds per side or till golden; turn once. Dust with powdered sugar. Makes 64.

Pick-a-Flavor Fritters

1 **cup all-purpose flour**
1 **tablespoon sugar**
1 **tablespoon baking powder**
¼ **teaspoon salt**
½ **cup milk**
1 **egg**
1 **tablespoon cooking oil**
  Desired Flavor Variation (see
    below)
  Shortening *or* cooking oil for
    deep-fat frying
  Butter *or* margarine *or* maple-
    flavored syrup (optional)

In mixing bowl stir together the flour, sugar, baking powder, and salt; set aside. Combine the milk, egg, and 1 tablespoon cooking oil; stir in the desired Flavor Variation chosen from below. Add milk mixture to the flour mixture, stirring just till moistened; do not beat smooth.

Drop batter by tablespoonfuls into deep, hot fat (375°). Fry 4 or 5 at a time, for 2 to 2½ minutes per side or till done, turning once. Drain on paper toweling.

Serve the fritters hot with butter, margarine, or maple-flavored syrup, if desired. Makes about 16 fritters.

Flavor Variations: 1) Add 1 cup chopped peeled *apple* plus ½ teaspoon *apple pie spice*. 2) Add 1 cup chopped peeled *pear* or *banana* plus ½ teaspoon *ground nutmeg*. 3) Add 1 cup diced fully cooked *ham* plus 1 teaspoon *dry mustard*. 4) Add one 8¾-ounce can whole kernel *corn*, drained, plus ½ teaspoon *onion salt* or 1 *green onion*, sliced. 5) Add 4 slices *bacon*, crisp-cooked, drained, and crumbled (substitute 1 tablespoon *bacon drippings* for the 1 tablespoon cooking oil).

Impress your family with an assortment of homemade doughnuts. Just make a
batch of light, tender *Cake Doughnuts* (see recipe, page 62) and top with a variety of glazes.

Coffee Cakes and Sweet Rolls

Fruit-Filled Ladder Loaf (pictured on pages 54 and 55)

1 3-ounce package cream cheese
¼ cup butter *or* margarine
2 cups Homemade Biscuit Mix
   (see recipe, page 81)*
½ cup chopped pecans
¼ cup milk*
½ of a 12-ounce can cherry *or*
   apricot cake and pastry filling
   Confectioners' Icing (see
   recipe, page 34)

In mixing bowl cut cream cheese and butter or margarine into Homemade Biscuit Mix till crumbly. Add nuts and milk; mix well. Knead on lightly floured surface for 8 to 10 strokes. Roll dough into a 12x8-inch rectangle on waxed paper. Turn onto greased baking sheet; remove paper. Spread filling lengthwise down center third of dough. Make 2½-inch cuts at 1-inch intervals on both long sides. Fold strips over filling, pinching into narrow points at center. Bake in 425° oven about 15 minutes or till done. Drizzle with Confectioners' Icing while warm. Makes 1 loaf.

*Note: You can substitute 2 cups *packaged biscuit mix* for the Homemade Biscuit Mix, *except* increase the milk to ⅓ *cup* liquid.

Cocoa Ripple Ring

¾ cup granulated sugar
½ cup shortening
2 eggs
1½ cups all-purpose flour
2 teaspoons baking powder
⅔ cup milk
⅓ cup presweetened cocoa
   powder
⅓ cup chopped walnuts
   Sifted powdered sugar
   (optional)

Cream together granulated sugar and shortening till light. Add eggs; beat well. Stir together flour, baking powder, and ¾ teaspoon *salt*. Add flour mixture and milk alternately to creamed mixture, beating till smooth after each addition.

Spoon ⅓ of the batter (1 cup) into greased 9-inch fluted tube pan or 6½-cup ring mold or 9x9x2-inch baking pan. Combine presweetened cocoa powder and nuts; sprinkle *half* over batter. Repeat layers, ending with batter. Bake in 350° oven 30 to 35 minutes. Cool in pan 5 minutes; turn out onto serving platter. Dust with sifted powdered sugar, if desired. Serve warm. Makes 1 coffee cake.

Rhubarb-Strawberry Coffee Cake

   Rhubarb-Strawberry Filling
3 cups all-purpose flour
1 cup sugar
1 teaspoon salt
1 teaspoon baking soda
1 teaspoon baking powder
1 cup butter *or* margarine
1 cup buttermilk *or* sour milk
2 slightly beaten eggs
1 teaspoon vanilla
¾ cup sugar
½ cup all-purpose flour
¼ cup butter *or* margarine

Prepare Rhubarb-Strawberry Filling; set aside to cool. In large mixing bowl stir together the 3 cups flour, the 1 cup sugar, salt, baking soda, and baking powder. Cut in the 1 cup butter or margarine till mixture resembles fine crumbs. Beat together buttermilk, eggs, and vanilla; add to flour-butter mixture. Stir just till moistened. Spread *half* the batter in a greased 13x9x2-inch baking pan.

Spread *cooled* Rhubarb-Strawberry Filling over batter in baking pan. Spoon remaining batter in small mounds atop fruit filling. Combine ¾ cup sugar and ½ cup flour; cut in the ¼ cup butter or margarine till mixture resembles fine crumbs. Sprinkle crumb mixture over batter. Bake in 350° oven for 40 to 45 minutes. Makes 1 coffee cake.

Rhubarb-Strawberry Filling: In saucepan combine 3 cups fresh *or* frozen cut-up *rhubarb* and one 16-ounce package frozen sliced *strawberries*. Cover and cook rhubarb and strawberries about 5 minutes. Stir in 2 tablespoons *lemon juice*. Combine 1 cup *sugar* and ⅓ cup *cornstarch*; add to rhubarb mixture. Cook and stir 4 to 5 minutes more or till thickened and bubbly.

Applesauce Coffee Cake

1¾ cups all-purpose flour
½ cup sugar
½ cup butter *or* margarine
2 beaten eggs
1 teaspoon vanilla
1½ teaspoons baking powder
½ teaspoon baking soda
1 cup chunk-style applesauce
¼ cup chopped nuts
½ teaspoon ground cinnamon

In mixing bowl stir together ¾ *cup* of the flour and the sugar; cut in butter or margarine till crumbly. Set aside ½ *cup* of the crumb mixture for topping. To remaining crumb mixture, add beaten eggs and vanilla; beat by hand till smooth.

Stir together remaining 1 cup flour, the baking powder, soda, and ½ teaspoon *salt*. Add flour mixture and applesauce alternately to creamed mixture, stirring after each addition. Turn into greased 8x8x2-inch baking pan. Stir nuts and cinnamon into reserved crumb topping; sprinkle atop coffee cake. Bake in 375° oven 30 minutes or till done. Serve warm. Makes 1 coffee cake.

Biscuit Bubble Ring (pictured on pages 54 and 55)

1 3-ounce package cream cheese, chilled
2 cups all-purpose flour
2 tablespoons granulated sugar
4 teaspoons baking powder
½ teaspoon salt
⅓ cup shortening
⅔ cup milk
¼ cup granulated sugar
½ teaspoon ground cinnamon
5 tablespoons butter *or* margarine, melted
⅓ cup chopped pecans
¼ cup light corn syrup
2 tablespoons brown sugar
2 tablespoons butter *or* margarine

Cut cream cheese into 20 equal cubes; set aside. In large mixing bowl stir together the flour, 2 tablespoons granulated sugar, baking powder, and salt. Cut in shortening till mixture resembles coarse crumbs. Make a well in center; add milk all at once. Stir just till dough clings together.

Turn dough out onto lightly floured surface. Knead gently for 10 to 12 strokes. Divide dough into 20 equal portions; pat *each* into a 2½- to 3-inch round.

Combine the ¼ cup granulated sugar and cinnamon. Place a cream cheese cube and ¼ *teaspoon* of the sugar-cinnamon mixture on *each* dough round. Bring up edges of dough and pinch edges to seal. Pour *3 tablespoons* of the melted butter or margarine into the bottom of a 5½-cup ring mold; turn mold to coat sides. Sprinkle *half* the chopped nuts and *half* the remaining sugar-cinnamon mixture into the mold.

Roll filled biscuits in remaining 2 tablespoons melted butter. Place *half* the biscuits, seam side up, atop sugar-nut mixture in mold. Repeat layers, using the remaining chopped nuts, sugar-cinnamon mixture, and filled biscuits.

Bake in 375° oven about 25 minutes or till golden. Cool 5 minutes in pan; invert pan onto serving platter.

Meanwhile, in small saucepan combine the corn syrup, brown sugar, and the 2 tablespoons butter or margarine. Heat until sugar is dissolved, stirring constantly. Drizzle sugar mixture over warm coffee cake. Makes 1 coffee cake.

Spicy Buttermilk Coffee Cake

2½ cups all-purpose flour
2 cups packed brown sugar
⅔ cup shortening
2 teaspoons baking powder
½ teaspoon baking soda
½ teaspoon ground cinnamon
½ teaspoon ground nutmeg
1 cup buttermilk *or* sour milk
2 beaten eggs
⅓ cup chopped nuts

Combine flour, brown sugar, and ½ teaspoon *salt*. Cut in shortening till mixture is crumbly; set aside ½ *cup* crumb mixture. To remaining crumb mixture add baking powder, soda, and spices; mix well. Add buttermilk or sour milk and eggs; mix well. Pour into two greased 8x1½-inch or 9x1½-inch round baking pans. Combine reserved crumbs with nuts; sprinkle atop cakes. Bake in 375° oven for 20 to 25 minutes. Serve warm. Makes 2 coffee cakes.

Peanut Butter Coffee Cake

½ **cup packed brown sugar**
½ **cup all-purpose flour**
¼ **cup peanut butter**
2 **tablespoons butter** *or*
   margarine, melted
½ **cup peanut butter**
¼ **cup shortening**
1 **cup packed brown sugar**
2 **eggs**
2 **cups all-purpose flour**
2 **teaspoons baking powder**
½ **teaspoon baking soda**
1 **cup milk**

In mixing bowl stir together ½ cup brown sugar, ½ cup flour, ¼ cup peanut butter, and melted butter or margarine till crumbly; set aside. Cream ½ cup peanut butter and shortening. Gradually beat in 1 cup brown sugar. Add eggs, one at a time, beating till light and fluffy after each addition.

Stir together 2 cups flour, baking powder, baking soda, and ½ teaspoon *salt*. Add flour mixture and milk alternately to creamed mixture, mixing well after each addition. Turn mixture into greased 13x9x2-inch baking pan. Sprinkle with crumbly topping. Bake in 375° oven for 30 to 35 minutes or till done. Makes 1 coffee cake.

Any-Fruit Coffee Cake

4 **cups chopped apples, apricots,**
   peaches, pineapple,
   blueberries, *or* **raspberries**
2 **tablespoons lemon juice**
1¼ **cups sugar**
⅓ **cup cornstarch**
3 **cups all-purpose flour**
1 **cup sugar**
1 **tablespoon baking powder**
1 **teaspoon ground cinnamon**
¼ **teaspoon ground mace**
1 **cup butter** *or* **margarine**
2 **slightly beaten eggs**
1 **cup milk**
1 **teaspoon vanilla**
½ **cup sugar**
½ **cup all-purpose flour**
¼ **cup butter** *or* **margarine**
½ **cup chopped walnuts**

In a saucepan combine choice of fruit and 1 cup *water*. Simmer, covered, about 5 minutes or till fruit is tender. Stir in lemon juice. Mix the 1¼ cups sugar and cornstarch; stir into fruit mixture. Cook and stir till thickened. Cool.

In mixing bowl stir together the 3 cups flour, 1 cup sugar, baking powder, cinnamon, mace, and 1 teaspoon *salt*. Cut in the 1 cup butter or margarine till mixture resembles fine crumbs. Combine eggs, milk, and vanilla. Add to flour mixture, mixing till blended. Spread *half* of the batter in greased 13x9x2-inch baking pan or two greased 8x8x2-inch baking pans.

Spread the cooled fruit mixture over the batter. Spoon the remaining batter in small mounds over fruit mixture, spreading out as much as possible. Combine the ½ cup sugar and ½ cup flour; cut in the ¼ cup butter or margarine till mixture resembles coarse crumbs. Stir in nuts. Sprinkle nut mixture over batter in pan. Bake in 350° oven 45 to 50 minutes for 13x9x2-inch pan (40 to 45 minutes for two 8x8x2-inch baking pans) or till cake tests done. Cool. Makes 1 large coffee cake or 2 small coffee cakes.

Orange-Date Coffee Cake

2 **cups all-purpose flour**
½ **cup granulated sugar**
1 **tablespoon baking powder**
1 **beaten egg**
½ **cup milk**
½ **cup cooking oil**
½ **cup snipped pitted dates**
2 **teaspoons finely shredded**
   orange peel
½ **cup orange juice**
½ **cup chopped walnuts**
½ **cup packed brown sugar**
2 **tablespoons butter** *or*
   margarine, softened
1 **teaspoon ground cinnamon**

Stir together flour, granulated sugar, baking powder, and ½ teaspoon *salt*. Make a well in the center. Combine egg, milk, and oil; add all at once to dry ingredients. Stir just till well mixed. Combine dates, orange peel, and orange juice; stir into batter just till blended. Spread evenly in greased 11x7x1½-inch baking pan. Combine walnuts, brown sugar, butter or margarine, and cinnamon; sprinkle over batter. Bake in 375° oven about 30 minutes. Makes 1 coffee cake.

Bran-Apple Coffee Cake

  1 **cup flour**
 ½ **cup packed brown sugar**
  1 **teaspoon ground cinnamon**
 ½ **cup butter** *or* **margarine**
  1 **cup whole bran cereal**
1½ **cups granulated sugar**
 ⅓ **cup butter** *or* **margarine**
  2 **eggs**
  1 **cup buttermilk** *or* **sour milk**
  1 **8-ounce can (1 cup) applesauce**
2½ **cups all-purpose flour**
  2 **cups whole bran cereal**
2½ **teaspoons baking soda**

In mixing bowl combine the 1 cup flour, brown sugar, and cinnamon. Cut in ½ cup butter or margarine till mixture resembles coarse crumbs; set aside for topping. In another bowl combine the 1 cup bran cereal and 1 cup *boiling water*; set aside. In a large mixer bowl cream the granulated sugar and the ⅓ cup butter or margarine. Beat in eggs. Add buttermilk or sour milk, applesauce, and softened bran mixture; mix well. Stir together the 2½ cups flour, 2 cups bran, baking soda, and ½ teaspoon *salt*; add to applesauce-bran mixture. Mix well. Pour into two greased 9x9x2-inch baking pans. Sprinkle *half* of the topping over each. Bake in 400° oven for 30 to 35 minutes. Makes 2 coffee cakes.

Blueberry Buckle

 ¾ **cup sugar**
 ½ **cup shortening**
  1 **egg**
2½ **cups all-purpose flour**
2½ **teaspoons baking powder**
 ½ **cup milk**
  2 **cups blueberries**
 ½ **cup sugar**
 ½ **teaspoon ground cinnamon**
 ¼ **cup butter** *or* **margarine**

Cream ¾ cup sugar and shortening till light and fluffy. Add egg; beat well. Stir together *2 cups* of the flour, the baking powder, and ¼ teaspoon *salt*. Add flour mixture and milk alternately to creamed mixture. Beat till smooth after each addition. Spread in greased 8x8x2-inch or 9x9x2-inch baking pan. Top with blueberries. Combine ½ cup sugar, the remaining ½ cup flour, and cinnamon; cut in butter or margarine till crumbly. Sprinkle over berries. Bake in 350° oven for 45 to 50 minutes. Cut into squares. Serve warm. Makes 1 coffee cake.

Quick Orange-Yogurt Coffee Cake

  1 **beaten egg**
  1 **8-ounce carton orange yogurt**
  1 **package 1-layer-size yellow** **cake mix**
 ½ **cup raisins**
  3 **tablespoons sugar**
 ½ **teaspoon ground cinnamon**

In mixing bowl combine egg and yogurt; add cake mix. Stir till combined. Stir in raisins. Turn into greased 8x8x2-inch baking pan. Combine sugar and cinnamon; sprinkle over top. Bake in 350° oven for 30 minutes or till done. Makes 1.

Streusel Coffee Cake

1½ **cups all-purpose flour**
 ¾ **cup granulated sugar**
  2 **teaspoons baking powder**
  1 **beaten egg**
 ½ **cup milk**
 ¼ **cup cooking oil**
 ½ **cup raisins (optional)**
 ½ **cup chopped nuts**
 ¼ **cup packed brown sugar**
  1 **tablespoon all-purpose flour**
  1 **tablespoon butter, softened**
  1 **teaspoon ground cinnamon**

Stir together the 1½ cups flour, granulated sugar, baking powder, and ½ teaspoon *salt*. Combine egg, milk, and oil. Add to flour mixture; mix well. Stir in raisins, if desired. Turn into greased 9x9x2-inch baking pan. Combine nuts, brown sugar, 1 tablespoon flour, butter, and cinnamon; sprinkle over batter. Bake in 375° oven about 25 minutes. Makes 1 coffee cake.

Apple Butter Rolls

2 **cups all-purpose flour**
4 **teaspoons baking powder**
1 **tablespoon sugar**
½ **teaspoon salt**
½ **cup shortening**
⅔ **cup milk**
1 **tablespoon butter *or* margarine,**
   softened
½ **cup apple butter**
½ **cup raisins**
¼ **cup apple butter**
¼ **cup sugar**
¼ **teaspoon ground cinnamon**

In mixing bowl stir together flour, baking powder, 1 table-spoon sugar, and salt. Cut in shortening till mixture resembles coarse crumbs. Add milk, stirring just till moistened. Knead on lightly floured surface for 8 to 10 strokes. Roll dough into a 16x8-inch rectangle.

Spread with softened butter or margarine. Combine ½ cup apple butter and raisins; spread evenly over dough. Roll up jelly-roll-style, beginning with long side. Seal seam well. Cut into 1-inch slices. Place, cut side down, in greased 8x8x2-inch baking pan. Spread surface of rolls with ¼ cup sugar and cinnamon; sprinkle over top. Bake in 375° oven for 30 to 35 minutes. Remove from pan. Serve warm. Makes 16 rolls.

Lemon Sticky Buns

½ **cup sugar**
⅓ **cup dark corn syrup**
¼ **cup butter *or* margarine**
1 **teaspoon finely shredded lemon**
   peel
2 **tablespoons lemon juice**
¾ **cup toasted sliced almonds**
3 **cups all-purpose flour**
¼ **cup sugar**
4 **teaspoons baking powder**
1 **teaspoon salt**
½ **cup shortening**
2 **beaten eggs**
⅔ **cup milk**
1 **tablespoon butter *or* margarine,**
   melted
¼ **cup sugar**
¼ **teaspoon ground nutmeg**

In small saucepan combine ½ cup sugar, corn syrup, ¼ cup butter or margarine, lemon peel, and lemon juice. Cook and stir till sugar dissolves and mixture boils. Pour into 13x9x2-inch baking pan. Sprinkle with toasted almonds.

Stir together flour, ¼ cup sugar, baking powder, and salt. Cut in shortening till mixture resembles coarse crumbs. Combine eggs and milk; add all at once to flour mixture. Stir just till dough clings together. Knead gently on lightly floured surface for 8 to 10 strokes. Roll into a 15x8-inch rectangle. Brush with the 1 tablespoon butter or margarine. Combine ¼ cup sugar and nutmeg; sprinkle over dough. Roll up jelly-roll-style, beginning with long side. Seal edge. Cut into 1-inch slices. Place, cut side down, atop syrup mixture in pan. Bake in 375° oven about 25 minutes. Immediately loosen sides and turn out onto wire rack. Serve warm. Makes 15 rolls.

Orange Caramel Rolls

¾ **cup sugar**
3 **tablespoons butter *or* margarine**
1 **tablespoon finely shredded**
   orange peel
2 **tablespoons orange juice**
2 **cups all-purpose flour**
1 **tablespoon baking powder**
½ **teaspoon salt**
⅓ **cup shortening**
¾ **cup milk**
¼ **cup sugar**
½ **teaspoon ground cinnamon**

In small saucepan combine the ¾ cup sugar, butter, orange peel, and orange juice. Bring to boiling over medium heat; cook and stir 1 minute. Set aside *2 tablespoons* orange mixture; pour remainder into 8x8x2-inch baking pan. Stir together flour, baking powder, and salt. Cut in shortening till mixture resembles coarse crumbs. Make a well in center. Add milk all at once, stirring just till dough clings together. Turn dough out onto lightly floured surface. Knead dough gently 15 to 20 strokes. Roll dough into a 12x9-inch rectangle. Spread dough with the reserved orange mixture. Mix the ¼ cup sugar and cinnamon; sprinkle over dough. Roll up jelly-roll-style, beginning with long side. Slice into 9 pieces. Place, cut side down, atop orange mixture in pan. Bake in 425° oven about 20 minutes or till golden. Loosen sides; invert onto serving plate. Serve warm. Makes 9.

Honey-Peanut Rolls

¼ **cup honey**
¼ **cup peanuts**
¼ **cup light raisins**
2 **tablespoons butter, melted**
¼ **teaspoon ground cardamom**
1 **package (10) refrigerated biscuits**

Combine honey, peanuts, raisins, melted butter or margarine, and cardamom; pour into an 8x1½-inch round baking pan. Arrange refrigerated biscuits in a single layer atop honey-peanut mixture. Bake in 375° oven about 20 minutes or till golden brown. Invert onto serving plate. Serve warm. Makes 10 rolls.

Sticky Nut Rolls

½ **cup light corn syrup** *or* **maple-flavored syrup**
⅓ **cup packed brown sugar**
3 **tablespoons butter** *or* **margarine, melted**
1 **tablespoon water**
⅓ **cup coarsely chopped pecans** *or* **walnuts**
2 **cups all-purpose flour**
1 **tablespoon baking powder**
½ **teaspoon salt**
⅓ **cup shortening**
¾ **cup milk**
¼ **cup granulated sugar**
½ **teaspoon ground cinnamon**

In saucepan combine syrup, brown sugar, butter or margarine, and water. Cook and stir over low heat till brown sugar is dissolved; do not boil. Spread in bottom of 9x9x2-inch baking pan. Sprinkle nuts over.

In mixing bowl stir together flour, baking powder, and salt. Cut in shortening till mixture resembles coarse crumbs. Make a well in center. Add milk all at once, stirring just till dough clings together. Turn dough out onto lightly floured surface. Knead dough gently 15 to 20 strokes. Roll into a 12x10-inch rectangle. Combine granulated sugar and cinnamon; sprinkle over dough. Roll up jelly-roll-style, beginning with long side. Slice into 1-inch slices. Place, cut side down, in prepared pan. Bake in 425° oven 30 minutes or till golden. Loosen sides and invert onto serving plate. Serve warm. Makes 12 rolls.

Easy Cinnamon Twists

1 **package (10) refrigerated biscuits**
2 **tablespoons butter, melted**
¼ **cup sugar**
1 **teaspoon ground cinnamon**
1 **tablespoon chopped walnuts**

On lightly floured surface, roll each biscuit into a 9-inch rope. Pinch ends together to form a circle. Dip biscuit circles in melted butter, then in mixture of sugar and cinnamon. Twist each biscuit to form a figure 8. Place biscuits on ungreased baking sheet. Sprinkle with nuts. Bake in 425° oven 8 to 10 minutes. Serve warm. Makes 10.

Quick Caramel-Pecan Rolls

¼ **cup packed brown sugar**
2 **teaspoons all-purpose flour**
2 **tablespoons butter** *or* **margarine**
2 **teaspoons milk**
½ **teaspoon rum extract**
1 **package (8) refrigerated crescent rolls**
1 **tablespoon butter** *or* **margarine, melted**
¼ **cup packed brown sugar**
2 **tablespoons chopped pecans**

For caramel sauce, in small saucepan combine ¼ cup brown sugar and the flour. Stir in 2 tablespoons butter and milk. Cook, stirring constantly, over medium heat till thickened and bubbly. Remove from heat; stir in rum extract. Divide mixture evenly among 8 muffin cups; set aside.

Unroll refrigerated rolls, separating into triangles. Brush each triangle with a little of the 1 tablespoon melted butter. Combine the ¼ cup packed brown sugar and nuts; sprinkle each roll with some nut mixture. Roll triangles up, *beginning at the point* and rolling to the top. Cut one roll-up in half crosswise; place both halves, cut side down, together in prepared muffin cup. Repeat with remaining rolls. (Fill any empty cups with a little water to prevent scorching. Bake in 375° oven about 15 minutes. Immediately invert onto wire rack. Serve warm. Makes 8.

Muffins, Biscuits, and Corn Bread

Basic Muffins

1¾ **cups all-purpose flour**
¼ **cup sugar**
2½ **teaspoons baking powder**
¾ **teaspoon salt**
1 **beaten egg**
¾ **cup milk**
⅓ **cup cooking oil**

In large mixing bowl stir together the flour, sugar, baking powder, and salt (step 1). Make a well in the center (step 2). Combine egg, milk, and oil. Add egg mixture all at once to flour mixture (step 3). Stir just till moistened; batter should be lumpy (step 4). Spoon into greased or paper-bake-cup-lined muffin cups, filling each about ⅔ full (step 5). Bake in 400° oven for 20 to 25 minutes or till golden. Remove from pans; serve warm. Makes 10 to 12 muffins.

Self-Rising Muffins: Prepare Basic Muffin batter as above, *except* substitute 1¾ cups *self-rising all-purpose flour* for the all-purpose flour; omit the baking powder and salt.

Blueberry Muffins: Prepare Basic Muffin batter as above. Combine ¾ cup fresh *or* frozen *blueberries*, thawed, and 2 *tablespoons* additional sugar. Add 1 teaspoon finely shredded *lemon peel*, if desired. Carefully fold into batter.

Cranberry Muffins: Prepare Basic Muffin batter as above. Coarsely chop 1 cup fresh *or* frozen *cranberries*; combine with ¼ cup additional sugar. Carefully fold into batter.

Apple-Raisin Muffins; Prepare Basic Muffin batter as above, *except* stir ½ teaspoon *ground cinnamon* into the flour mixture. Carefully fold 1 cup chopped peeled *apple* and ¼ cup *raisins* into batter.

Jelly Muffins: Prepare Basic Muffin batter as above. Spoon 1 teaspoon *jelly* atop batter in *each* muffin cup before baking.

Date-Nut Muffins: Prepare Basic Muffin batter as above. Fold ⅔ cup coarsely chopped pitted *dates* and ⅓ cup chopped *walnuts or pecans* into the batter.

Cheese Muffins: Prepare Basic Muffin batter as above, *except* stir ½ cup shredded *Swiss or cheddar cheese* into flour mixture.

Ham 'n Cheesers: Prepare Basic Muffin batter as above, *except* stir ½ cup finely chopped, fully cooked *ham* into the egg mixture. Stir ½ cup shredded *cheese* (2 ounces) and ½ teaspoon *dry mustard* into the flour mixture.

Bacon Muffins: Prepare Basic Muffin batter as above, *except* cook 4 slices *bacon* till crisp; drain and crumble, reserving drippings. Combine bacon drippings with enough cooking oil to make ⅓ *cup* total mixture; use in place of the ⅓ cup cooking oil. Carefully fold bacon into batter.

Banana-Nut Muffins: Prepare Basic Muffin batter as above, *except* decrease milk to ½ *cup*. Stir 1 cup mashed *banana* and ½ cup chopped *nuts* into batter.

Pumpkin Muffins: Prepare Basic Muffin batter as above, *except* increase sugar to ⅓ *cup*. Add ½ cup canned *pumpkin* to the egg mixture. Stir ½ teaspoon *each ground cinnamon* and *ground nutmeg* into flour mixture. Stir ½ cup *raisins* into batter.

Apple-and-Spice Muffins: Prepare Basic Muffin batter as above, *except* stir ½ teaspoon *ground cinnamon* into flour mixture. Add 1 cup chopped, peeled *apple* with the egg mixture; stir just till moistened. Mix 2 tablespoons *sugar* and ½ teaspoon *ground cinnamon*; sprinkle mixture over muffins before baking.

1

In large mixing bowl thoroughly stir together the flour, sugar, baking powder, and salt (sifting is not necessary).

To make mixing easier, sprinkle the baking powder and salt over the surface of the flour instead of pouring it all in one spot.

2

Gently push flour mixture against edges of bowl to make a well in the center. Use a wooden spoon for this.

3

Add egg-milk-oil mixture to flour mixture all at once, pouring into the well.

4

Stir mixture just till moistened. It should appear lumpy; do not try to beat till smooth. Such overmixing will result in muffins that are peaked and smooth on top, with a tough, heavy texture and holes or tunnels.

5

Grease bottoms *only* of muffin cups. If sides are greased, muffins will rise unevenly and form a rim. Or, line pans with paper bake cups as recipe directs.

Fill prepared muffin cups only ⅔ full to allow space for rising and to yield perfect-size muffins. An easy way to fill muffin cups is to push the batter from the spoon with a rubber spatula.

Adding Berries

When adding berries to muffin batter, begin by stirring the batter just till moistened; the batter should be lumpy. Then, carefully fold in the desired berries. Using this method, fruit such as blueberries will not "bleed" and discolor or break down in the batter.

Rhubarb Muffins

2 cups finely chopped rhubarb
¾ cup granulated sugar
1 teaspoon grated orange peel
2½ cups all-purpose flour
1½ teaspoons baking powder
1 teaspoon baking soda
2 beaten eggs
¾ cup buttermilk *or* sour milk
3 tablespoons butter, melted

Combine rhubarb, ¼ *cup* of the granulated sugar, and orange peel; let stand 5 minutes. In mixing bowl stir together flour, the remaining ½ cup granulated sugar, baking powder, soda, and ½ teaspoon *salt*; make a well in center. Combine eggs, buttermilk or sour milk, and melted butter. Add all at once to dry ingredients, stirring just till moistened (batter should be lumpy). Gently fold in rhubarb mixture. Fill greased or paper-bake-cup-lined muffin cups ⅔ full. Bake in 375° oven 20 to 25 minutes. Makes 16 to 18 muffins.

Sunshine Muffins

1 8-ounce can crushed pineapple
Milk
1½ cups Homemade Biscuit Mix (see recipe, page 81) *or* packaged biscuit mix
3 tablespoons sugar
1 beaten egg
1 tablespoon sugar
1 tablespoon finely shredded orange peel

Drain pineapple, reserving syrup. Add enough milk to syrup to measure ¾ cup liquid. Combine Homemade Biscuit Mix or packaged biscuit mix and the 3 tablespoons sugar. Combine egg, the reserved pineapple liquid, and ¼ cup drained pineapple; add all at once to dry ingredients, stirring just till moistened. Fill greased or paper-bake-cup-lined muffin cups ⅔ full. Stir together remaining drained pineapple, 1 tablespoon sugar, and orange peel. Spoon about *1 tablespoon* pineapple mixture atop batter in *each* muffin cup. Bake in 400° oven 20 to 25 minutes. Makes 8 to 10.

Orange-Oatmeal Muffins

1 orange
1 cup all-purpose flour
¼ cup sugar
1 tablespoon baking powder
1 cup quick-cooking rolled oats
1 beaten egg
¼ cup milk
3 tablespoons cooking oil
2 tablespoons sugar
1 tablespoon all-purpose flour
1 teaspoon butter, melted
¼ teaspoon ground cinnamon

Finely shred enough peel from orange to measure *1 teaspoon*. Squeeze enough juice from orange to measure ½ *cup* juice.

In mixing bowl stir together 1 cup flour, ¼ cup sugar, baking powder, and ½ teaspoon *salt*. Stir in rolled oats; make a well in the center. Combine egg, milk, oil, orange peel, and orange juice; add all at once to dry ingredients, stirring just till moistened (batter should be lumpy). Fill greased or paper-bake-cup-lined muffin cups ⅔ full. Combine 2 tablespoons sugar, 1 tablespoon flour, melted butter, and cinnamon; sprinkle over batter in muffin cups. Bake in 400° oven about 15 minutes or till golden brown. Makes 12 muffins.

Cinnamon-Graham Muffins

1 beaten egg
¾ cup buttermilk *or* sour milk
¼ cup cooking oil
1 teaspoon vanilla
1½ cups finely crushed cinnamon graham crackers
½ cup raisins
¾ cup all-purpose flour
2 tablespoons sugar
2 teaspoons baking powder
½ teaspoon baking soda

In large bowl combine egg, buttermilk, cooking oil, and vanilla. Stir in cracker crumbs and raisins; set aside. Stir together flour, sugar, baking powder, baking soda, and ¼ teaspoon *salt*. Add to egg mixture, stirring just till moistened (batter should be lumpy). Fill greased or paper-bake-cup-lined muffin cups ⅔ full. Bake in 400° oven 20 to 25 minutes or till done. Makes 10 to 12 muffins.

Carrot Muffins (pictured on the cover)

1 cup all-purpose flour
¼ cup packed brown sugar
2 teaspoons baking powder
2 beaten eggs
1 cup finely shredded carrot
¼ cup cooking oil
1 tablespoon lemon juice

In mixing bowl stir together flour, brown sugar, baking powder, and ½ teaspoon *salt*; make a well in center. Combine eggs, shredded carrot, cooking oil, and lemon juice; add all at once to dry ingredients, stirring just till moistened (batter should be lumpy). Fill greased or paper-bake-cup-lined muffin cups ¾ full. Bake in 375° oven about 25 minutes or till golden brown. Makes 8 muffins.

Upside-Down Branberry Muffins

1 beaten egg
1¼ cups milk
⅓ cup cooking oil
1½ cups whole bran cereal
½ cup packed brown sugar
¼ cup butter *or* margarine, melted
1 cup fresh *or* frozen cranberries, chopped
1¼ cups all-purpose flour
⅓ cup granulated sugar
1 tablespoon baking powder

In large bowl combine egg, milk, and cooking oil; stir in bran cereal. Let stand 5 minutes. Meanwhile, mix brown sugar and the melted butter or margarine. Place a *teaspoonful* of brown sugar mixture into *each* of 18 greased muffin cups. Sprinkle some of the cranberries into each. Stir together flour, granulated sugar, baking powder, and ½ teaspoon *salt*; add to bran mixture, stirring just till moistened (batter should be lumpy). Spoon batter atop cranberries. Bake in 400° oven for 20 to 25 minutes. Cool about ½ minute; turn out onto wire rack. Makes 18 muffins.

Whole Wheat-Banana Muffins

1 beaten egg
¾ cup milk
⅓ cup cooking oil
½ cup mashed ripe banana
1 cup all-purpose flour
½ cup whole wheat flour
¼ cup sugar
¼ cup wheat germ
2½ teaspoons baking powder
¼ teaspoon baking soda
¼ teaspoon ground cinnamon

In small mixing bowl combine egg, milk, and oil. Add banana; mix well. In large mixing bowl stir together all-purpose flour, whole wheat flour, sugar, wheat germ, baking powder, baking soda, cinnamon, and ¾ teaspoon *salt*. Make a well in the center. Add banana mixture all at once; stir just till moistened (batter should be lumpy). Spoon into greased or paper-bake-cup-lined muffin cups, filling each about ⅔ full. Bake in 375° oven for 20 to 25 minutes. Remove from pan; serve warm. Makes 12 muffins.

Easy Lemon-Blueberry Muffins (pictured on pages 54 and 55)

1 cup fresh *or* frozen blueberries
1 beaten egg
2 cups Homemade Biscuit Mix (see recipe, page 81) *or* packaged biscuit mix
⅓ cup sugar
2 tablespoons butter *or* margarine, softened
1 lemon
  Milk
  Melted butter *or* margarine
2 tablespoons sugar

Thaw blueberries, if frozen; drain. In mixing bowl combine egg, Homemade Biscuit Mix or packaged biscuit mix, ⅓ cup sugar, and 2 tablespoons softened butter or margarine. Finely shred enough peel from lemon to make *1 tablespoon*; set aside. Squeeze lemon; add enough milk to lemon juice to make ⅔ cup liquid. Add to biscuit-mix mixture; mix well. Gently fold in blueberries. Fill greased or paper-bake-cup-lined muffin cups ⅔ full.

Bake in 400° oven about 25 minutes. While warm, dip muffin tops in some melted butter or margarine, then in a mixture of 2 tablespoons sugar and the reserved lemon peel. Makes 12 muffins.

Honey-Wheat Muffins

1 **cup all-purpose flour**
½ **cup whole wheat flour**
2 **teaspoons baking powder**
1 **beaten egg**
½ **cup milk**
½ **cup honey**
¼ **cup cooking oil**
½ **teaspoon finely shredded lemon peel**

Stir together all-purpose flour, whole wheat flour, baking powder, and ½ teaspoon *salt*; make a well in center. Combine egg, milk, honey, oil, and lemon peel; add all at once to dry ingredients, stirring just till moistened (batter should be lumpy). Fill greased or paper-bake-cup-lined muffin cups ⅔ full. Bake in 375° oven about 20 minutes. Makes 10.

Sunflower Seed Muffins: Prepare Honey-Wheat Muffin batter as above, *except* stir ½ cup shelled *sunflower seed* into the flour mixture. Makes 12 muffins.

Granola Muffins

1 **cup granola**
½ **cup snipped dried apricots**
1¾ **cups all-purpose flour**
½ **cup sugar**
½ **cup chopped walnuts**
1 **tablespoon baking powder**
1 **beaten egg**
⅔ **cup milk**
½ **cup cooking oil**

In mixing bowl combine the granola and apricots; pour ½ cup *boiling water* over. Set aside.

In another bowl stir together the flour, sugar, chopped nuts, baking powder, and ½ teaspoon *salt*; make a well in center. Stir egg, milk, and oil into fruit mixture; add all at once to flour mixture, stirring just till moistened (batter should be lumpy). Spoon into greased or paper-bake-cup-lined muffin cups, filling ⅔ full. Bake in 375° oven for 20 to 25 minutes. Makes about 18 muffins.

French Breakfast Puffs

1½ **cups all-purpose flour**
1½ **teaspoons baking powder**
¼ **teaspoon ground nutmeg**
½ **cup sugar**
⅓ **cup shortening**
1 **egg**
½ **cup milk**
½ **cup sugar**
1 **teaspoon ground cinnamon**
6 **tablespoons butter, melted**

In mixing bowl stir together flour, baking powder, nutmeg, and ½ teaspoon *salt*; set aside. In mixer bowl cream together ½ cup sugar, the shortening, and egg. Add flour mixture and milk alternately to creamed mixture, beating well after each addition.

Fill 12 greased muffin cups ⅔ full. Bake in 350° oven for 20 to 25 minutes or till golden. Combine ½ cup sugar and the cinnamon. Remove muffins from oven; immediately dip in melted butter, then in sugar-cinnamon mixture till coated. Serve warm. Makes 12 muffins.

Pineapple-Lemon Upside-Down Muffins

½ **cup packed brown sugar**
3 **tablespoons butter, melted**
1 **teaspoon grated lemon peel**
⅛ **teaspoon ground nutmeg**
1 **8-ounce can pineapple slices, drained and cut up**
8 **maraschino cherries, halved**
2 **cups all-purpose flour**
¼ **cup granulated sugar**
1 **tablespoon baking powder**
⅛ **teaspoon ground nutmeg**
1 **beaten egg**
1 **cup milk**
3 **tablespoons cooking oil**

Combine brown sugar, melted butter, lemon peel, and ⅛ teaspoon nutmeg. Divide mixture evenly among 16 greased muffin cups. Arrange a few pineapple pieces and a cherry half in bottom of *each* cup. In mixing bowl throughly stir together flour, granulated sugar, baking powder, ⅛ teaspoon nutmeg, and ½ teaspoon *salt;* make a well in center. Combine egg, milk, and oil. Add all at once to dry ingredients, stirring just till dry ingredients are moistened (batter should be lumpy). Spoon into prepared muffin cups. Bake in 400° oven for 18 to 20 minutes or till done. Invert muffins onto wire rack to cool. Makes 16 muffins.

Plan a company-special breakfast around hearty apricot-filled *Granola Muffins,*
cinnamon-sugar-topped *French Breakfast Puffs,* and spicy *Pineapple-Lemon Upside-Down Muffins.*

Brownie Muffins

1¾ cups all-purpose flour
½ cup sugar
3 tablespoons unsweetened
   cocoa powder
2½ teaspoons baking powder
½ teaspoon ground cinnamon
1 beaten egg
¾ cup milk
⅓ cup cooking oil
⅓ cup chopped nuts

In mixing bowl stir together the flour, sugar, cocoa powder, baking powder, cinnamon, and ¾ teaspoon *salt*; make a well in center. Combine egg, milk, and oil; add all at once to dry ingredients, stirring just till moistened (batter should be lumpy). Fold in chopped nuts. Fill greased or paper-bake-cup-lined muffin cups ⅔ full. Bake in 400° oven for 18 to 20 minutes. Makes 12 muffins.

Coffee Cake Muffins

1½ cups all-purpose flour
½ cup granulated sugar
2 teaspoons baking powder
¼ cup shortening
1 beaten egg
½ cup milk
¼ cup packed brown sugar
¼ cup chopped walnuts *or* pecans
1 tablespoon all-purpose flour
1 tablespoon butter, softened
1 teaspoon ground cinnamon

In mixing bowl stir together 1½ cups flour, the granulated sugar, baking powder, and ½ teaspoon *salt*. Cut in shortening till mixture resembles coarse crumbs. Combine egg and milk; add all at once to flour mixture, stirring just till moistened (batter should be lumpy).
   Combine brown sugar, nuts, 1 tablespoon flour, butter, and cinnamon. Spoon *half* the batter into 12 greased or paper-bake-cup-lined muffin cups. Sprinkle with nut mixture; top with remaining batter, filling cups ½ full. Bake in 375° oven for 20 to 25 minutes. Makes 12 muffins.

Bran Muffins

1½ cups whole bran cereal
1 cup buttermilk *or* sour milk
1 beaten egg
¼ cup cooking oil *or* melted
   shortening
1 cup all-purpose flour
⅓ cup packed brown sugar
2 teaspoons baking powder
½ teaspoon baking soda
½ teaspoon salt
¾ cup raisins *or* snipped pitted
   dates (optional)

In mixing bowl combine bran cereal and buttermilk; let stand 3 minutes or till liquid is absorbed. Stir in egg and oil or melted shortening; set aside. In mixing bowl stir together the flour, brown sugar, baking powder, baking soda, and salt; make a well in the center. Add bran mixture all at once, stirring just till moistened (batter will be thick). If desired, gently fold in raisins or snipped dates. Fill greased muffin cups ⅔ full. Bake in 400° oven for 20 to 25 minutes. Makes 10 to 12 muffins.

Sausage Supper Muffins

8 ounces bulk pork sausage
1 cup all-purpose flour
1 cup yellow cornmeal
½ cup grated parmesan cheese
¼ cup sugar
4 teaspoons baking powder
2 beaten eggs
1 cup milk
¼ cup cooking oil

In skillet brown sausage, stirring to break into small pieces; drain off fat. Stir together flour, cornmeal, parmesan cheese, sugar, baking powder, and ¾ teaspoon *salt*; make a well in center. Combine eggs, milk, and oil; add all at once to dry ingredients, stirring just till moistened (batter should be lumpy). Fold in sausage. Fill greased muffin cups ⅔ full. Bake in 400° oven for 20 to 25 minutes or till golden. Makes 12 muffins.

Cornmeal-Cheese Muffins

1½ **cups all-purpose flour**
½ **cup yellow cornmeal**
¼ **cup sugar**
1 **tablespoon baking powder**
½ **cup shredded cheddar cheese**
1 **beaten egg**
1 **cup milk**
½ **cup cream-style cottage cheese**
¼ **cup cooking oil**

In mixing bowl stir together flour, cornmeal, sugar, baking powder, and ¾ teaspoon *salt*. Stir in shredded cheese; make a well in the center. Combine egg, milk, cottage cheese, and cooking oil; add all at once to dry ingredients, stirring just till moistened (batter should be lumpy). Fill well-greased muffin cups ⅔ full. Bake in 400° oven for 20 to 25 minutes. Let stand 3 or 4 minutes in pan. Loosen carefully; remove from pan. Makes 16 muffins.

Carrot-Pineapple Muffins

1 **8-ounce can crushed pineapple**
Milk
2 **cups all-purpose flour**
⅓ **cup packed brown sugar**
1 **tablespoon baking powder**
1 **beaten egg**
¾ **cup finely shredded carrot**
⅓ **cup cooking oil**
½ **teaspoon vanilla**
2 **tablespoons granulated sugar**
½ **teaspoon ground cinnamon**

Drain pineapple, reserving syrup; add enough milk to syrup to measure ¾ *cup* liquid. Stir together the flour, brown sugar, baking powder, and ½ teaspoon *salt*; make a well in the center. Combine egg, carrot, oil, vanilla, milk-syrup mixture, and drained pineapple; add all at once to dry ingredients, stirring just till moistened (batter should be lumpy). Fill greased or paper-bake-cup-lined muffin cups ⅔ full. Stir together granulated sugar and cinnamon; sprinkle atop muffins. Bake in 400° oven for 20 to 25 minutes. Makes 12 muffins.

Spiced Cranberry-Nut Muffins

1 **cup fresh or frozen cranberries**
¼ **cup sugar**
1¾ **cups all-purpose flour**
¼ **cup sugar**
1 **tablespoon baking powder**
½ **teaspoon ground cinnamon**
¼ **teaspoon ground allspice**
1 **beaten egg**
¼ **teaspoon grated orange peel**
¾ **cup orange juice**
⅓ **cup butter or margarine, melted**
¼ **cup chopped walnuts**

Coarsely chop cranberries. Toss cranberries with ¼ cup sugar; set aside. In mixing bowl stir together the flour, ¼ cup sugar, baking powder, cinnamon, allspice, and 1 teaspoon *salt*; make a well in center. Combine egg, orange peel, orange juice, and melted butter or margarine; add all at once to dry ingredients, stirring just till moistened (batter should be lumpy). Gently fold in cranberry mixture and nuts. Fill greased or paper-bake-cup-lined muffin cups ⅔ full. Bake in 400° oven for 20 to 25 minutes or till golden. Makes 12 muffins.

Apple Butter Muffins

2 **cups Homemade Biscuit Mix**
   (see recipe, page 81) or
   packaged biscuit mix
2 **tablespoons granulated sugar**
1 **beaten egg**
½ **cup milk**
2 **tablespoons cooking oil**
½ **cup chopped walnuts**
¼ **cup apple butter**
   Spicy Topping

In mixing bowl combine Homemade Biscuit Mix and granulated sugar. Combine egg, milk, and oil; add all at once to biscuit mixture, stirring just till moistened (batter should be lumpy). Stir in nuts. Fill 12 paper-bake-cup-lined muffin cups ⅓ full. Top *each* with *1 teaspoon* of the apple butter. Top with remaining batter. Sprinkle with Spicy Topping. Bake in 400° oven for 20 to 25 minutes. Makes 12.

Spicy Topping: Combine 2 tablespoons *brown sugar*, 1 tablespoon *all-purpose flour*, and ¼ teaspoon ground *cinnamon*. Cut in 2 teaspoons *butter or margarine* till crumbly.

Biscuits Supreme (pictured on page 83)

2 cups all-purpose flour
4 teaspoons baking powder
2 teaspoons sugar
½ teaspoon cream of tartar
½ teaspoon salt
½ cup shortening
⅔ cup milk

Stir together flour, baking powder, sugar, cream of tartar, and salt. Cut in shortening till mixture resembles coarse crumbs (step 1). Make a well in the center; add milk all at once. Stir just till dough clings together (step 2). Knead gently on lightly floured surface for 10 to 12 strokes (step 3). Roll or pat to ½-inch thickness. Cut with 2½-inch biscuit cutter*, dipping cutter in flour between cuts (step 4). Transfer to ungreased baking sheet (step 5). Bake in 450° oven for 10 to 12 minutes or till golden. Serve warm. Makes 10 to 12 biscuits.

Buttermilk Biscuits: Prepare Biscuits Supreme batter as above, *except* stir ¼ teaspoon *baking soda* into flour mixture and substitute ¾ cup *buttermilk* for the milk.

Cornmeal Biscuits: Prepare Biscuits Supreme batter as above, *except* use only 1½ cups all-purpose flour and add ½ cup yellow *cornmeal*. If desired, stir ¼ teaspoon *ground sage* into flour mixture.

Garden Biscuits: Prepare Biscuits Supreme batter as above, *except* add 2 tablespoons finely chopped *carrot*, 1 tablespoon finely snipped *parsley*, and 1 teaspoon finely chopped *green onion* to flour mixture with the milk.

Sour Cream Biscuits: Prepare Biscuits Supreme batter as above, *except* use 1 cup dairy *sour cream* and only 2 *tablespoons* milk.

*Note: If you do not have a biscuit cutter, pat dough into a ½-inch-thick rectangle. Cut into squares, triangles, or strips using a sharp knife.

1

After cutting in the shortening, the mixture should resemble coarse crumbs, as shown.

Avoid blending the fat completely with the flour or using a liquid shortening. These produce mealy biscuits rather than the flaky, tender ones that are more desirable.

2

Using a fork, stir the mixture quickly. Stir just till the dough follows the fork around the bowl and forms a soft dough, as shown. Too much mixing results in tough biscuits that are not as light as desired.

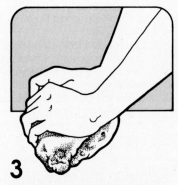

3

Knead gently on a floured surface for 10 to 12 strokes, as shown. This helps develop the biscuits' structure and evenly distributes the moisture to make biscuits more flaky.

For ease in kneading, curve fingers over dough, pull it toward you, then push it down and away from you with the heels of your hands. Give dough a quarter turn; fold toward you, and push down.

 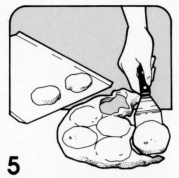 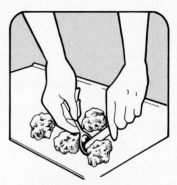

4

Cut dough with a 2½-inch biscuit cutter, as shown. Dip cutter in flour between cuts to prevent sticking. Press the cutter straight down to get straight-sided, evenly shaped biscuits. Be especially careful not to twist the cutter or flatten the cut biscuit edges.

5

Using a metal spatula, carefully transfer the cut biscuits to an ungreased baking sheet, as shown. For crusty-sided biscuits, place about 1 inch apart. For soft-sided biscuits, place biscuits close together in an ungreased baking pan.

Reroll scraps of dough and cut into more biscuit shapes.

Making Drop Biscuits

To make drop biscuits, use the biscuit recipe at left, *except* increase milk to *1 cup*. Combine ingredients as directed but *do not knead, roll, or cut.* Use a spatula to push dough from a tablespoon onto a greased baking sheet. Makes 12.

Homemade Biscuit Mix

- **10 cups all-purpose flour**
- **⅓ cup baking powder**
- **¼ cup sugar**
- **4 teaspoons salt**
- **2 cups shortening that does not require refrigeration**

In large mixing bowl stir together flour, baking powder, sugar, and salt. With pastry blender cut in shortening till mixture resembles coarse crumbs. Store in covered airtight container up to six weeks at room temperature. To use, spoon mix lightly into measuring cup; level off with a straight-edged spatula. (For longer storage, place in a sealed freezer container and store in the freezer for up to six months. To use, allow mix to come to room temperature.) Makes 12½ cups.

Biscuits: Place 2 cups *Homemade Biscuit Mix* in a bowl; make a well in center. Add ½ cup *milk*. Stir with fork just till dough follows fork around bowl. On lightly floured surface, knead dough 10 to 12 strokes. Roll or pat to ½-inch thickness. Cut dough with floured 2½-inch biscuit cutter. Bake on baking sheet in 450° oven 10 to 12 minutes. Makes 10.

Muffins: Combine 3 cups *Homemade Biscuit Mix* and 3 tablespoons *sugar*. Mix 1 beaten *egg* and 1 cup *milk*; add all at once to dry ingredients. Stir till moistened. Fill greased muffin cups ⅔ full. Bake in 400° oven for 20 to 25 minutes or till golden. Makes 12 muffins.

Pancakes: Place 2 cups *Homemade Biscuit Mix* in a bowl. Add 2 beaten *eggs* and 1 cup *milk* all at once to biscuit mix, stirring till blended but still slightly lumpy. Pour about ¼ *cup* batter onto hot, lightly greased griddle. Cook till golden brown, turning to cook other side. Makes 10.

Pecan Biscuit Spirals

2 cups all-purpose flour
2 tablespoons granulated sugar
1 tablespoon baking powder
½ teaspoon salt
½ cup butter *or* margarine
1 beaten egg
½ cup milk
1 tablespoon butter *or* margarine, melted
¼ cup finely chopped pecans
3 tablespoons brown sugar *or* granulated sugar
1 cup sifted powdered sugar (optional)
4 to 5 teaspoons milk (optional)

In mixing bowl stir together flour, 2 tablespoons granulated sugar, baking powder, and salt. Cut in ½ cup butter or margarine till mixture resembles coarse crumbs. Make a well in center. Combine egg and ½ cup milk; add all at once to dry mixture. Stir just till dough clings together. Knead gently on lightly floured surface for 12 to 15 strokes.

Roll dough into a 15x8-inch rectangle. Brush with 1 tablespoon melted butter. Combine pecans and 3 tablespoons brown or granulated sugar; sprinkle over dough. Fold dough in half lengthwise to make a 15x4-inch rectangle. Cut into fifteen 1-inch-wide strips. Holding a strip at both ends, twist in opposite directions twice, forming a spiral. Place on lightly greased baking sheet, pressing both ends down. Bake in 450° oven about 10 minutes. If desired, combine powdered sugar and 4 to 5 teaspoons milk till of drizzling consistency; drizzle over warm biscuit spirals. Makes 15 spirals.

Beer-Cheese Triangles

2 cups Homemade Biscuit Mix (see recipe, page 81) *or* packaged biscuit mix
½ cup shredded cheddar cheese (2 ounces)
½ cup beer

In mixing bowl stir together Homemade Biscuit Mix or packaged biscuit mix and shredded cheese. Make a well in center; add beer all at once. Stir just till mixture clings together. Knead gently on lightly floured surface for 5 strokes. Roll or pat dough into a 6-inch circle. Cut into 10 wedges. Place on greased baking sheet. Bake in 450° oven for 8 to 10 minutes or till golden. Makes 10 biscuits.

Whole Wheat Drop Biscuits

1 cup all-purpose flour
1 cup whole wheat flour
1 tablespoon baking powder
½ teaspoon salt
⅓ cup shortening
¼ cup shelled sunflower seed
1 beaten egg
1 cup milk

In mixing bowl thoroughly stir together the all-purpose flour, whole wheat flour, baking powder, and salt. Cut in shortening till mixture resembles coarse crumbs. Stir in sunflower seed. Combine egg and milk; add all at once to flour mixture. Stir quickly just till dough clings together. Drop from a tablespoon onto greased baking sheet. Bake in 450° oven for 12 to 15 minutes. Makes 12 to 14 biscuits.

Orange Pan Biscuits

1 cup all-purpose flour
2 teaspoons baking powder
1 teaspoon finely shredded orange peel
¼ teaspoon cream of tartar
¼ cup shortening
⅓ cup milk
2 tablespoons butter *or* margarine, melted
1 tablespoon sugar
¼ teaspoon ground nutmeg

In mixing bowl stir together flour, baking powder, shredded orange peel, cream of tartar, and ¼ teaspoon *salt*. Cut in shortening till mixture resembles coarse crumbs. Make a well in center; add milk all at once. Stir just till mixture clings together.

Divide dough into 8 pieces. With lightly floured hands, form each piece into a ball. Roll in melted butter or margarine; place in a 9-inch pie plate, spacing evenly. Combine sugar and nutmeg; sprinkle over dough. Bake in 450° oven about 15 minutes or till biscuits are golden brown. Serve warm. Makes 8 biscuits.

Serve tender, flaky biscuits at any meal. From the top are sweet *Pecan Biscuit Spirals,* light *Biscuits Supreme* (see recipe, page 80), and quick *Beer-Cheese Triangles.*

Oatmeal Scones

1 cup all-purpose flour
3 tablespoons sugar
2 teaspoons baking powder
6 tablespoons butter *or* margarine
1 cup quick-cooking rolled oats
½ cup dried currants *or* raisins, chopped
2 beaten eggs

In mixing bowl stir together flour, sugar, baking powder, and ¼ teaspoon *salt*. Cut in butter or margarine till mixture resembles coarse crumbs. Stir in oats and chopped currants or raisins. Stir in eggs till dry ingredients are moistened (dough will be sticky). On lightly floured surface, roll or pat dough into a 7-inch circle. Cut circle into 12 wedges. Place on baking sheet. Bake in 400° oven for 10 to 12 minutes or till golden brown. Makes 12 scones.

Spicy Raisin Drop Biscuits

2 cups all-purpose flour
¼ cup sugar
1 tablespoon baking powder
⅓ cup shortening
1 cup raisins
½ teaspoon finely shredded orange peel
1 beaten egg
1 cup milk
2 tablespoons sugar
¼ teaspoon ground cinnamon
⅛ teaspoon ground nutmeg
2 tablespoons butter, melted

Thoroughly stir together the flour, ¼ cup sugar, baking powder, and ½ teaspoon *salt*. Cut in shortening till mixture resembles coarse crumbs. Stir in raisins and orange peel. Make a well in center. Combine egg and milk; add all at once to dry mixture. Stir just till dough clings together. Using a *scant ¼ cup* of batter for each biscuit, push dough with a knife or narrow spatula onto greased baking sheet. Bake in 400° oven for 12 to 15 minutes. Meanwhile, combine 2 tablespoons sugar, cinnamon, and nutmeg. While biscuits are warm, brush tops with melted butter and sprinkle with sugar-spice mixture. Makes 16 to 18 biscuits.

Cheddar Cheese Biscuits

2 cups all-purpose flour
1 tablespoon baking powder
½ teaspoon salt
¼ cup shortening
1 beaten egg
¾ cup milk
½ cup shredded sharp cheddar cheese (2 ounces)
1 tablespoon butter *or* margarine, melted
Poppy seed *or* sesame seed

Stir together the flour, baking powder, and salt. Cut in shortening till mixture resembles coarse crumbs. Make a well in center. Combine egg and milk; add all at once to dry mixture. Add cheese. Stir just till dough clings together. Knead gently on lightly floured surface for 10 to 12 strokes. Roll or pat dough to ½-inch thickness. Cut with 2½-inch biscuit cutter; dip cutter in flour between cuts. Place on ungreased baking sheet. Brush tops with melted butter or margarine. Sprinkle with poppy or sesame seed. Bake in 450° oven for 10 to 12 minutes. Makes 10 biscuits.

Hush Puppies

1 beaten egg
1 cup buttermilk
½ cup finely chopped onion
1¾ cups cornmeal
½ cup all-purpose flour
1 tablespoon sugar
2 teaspoons baking powder
½ teaspoon baking soda
Shortening *or* cooking oil for deep-fat frying

In mixing bowl stir together egg, buttermilk, onion, and ¼ cup *water*; set aside. In large mixing bowl combine cornmeal, flour, sugar, baking powder, baking soda, and 1 teaspoon *salt*. Add egg mixture to cornmeal mixture; stir just till moistened. Drop batter by tablespoonfuls into deep hot fat (375°). Fry about 2 minutes or till golden brown, turning once. Drain on paper toweling. Serve hot with butter or margarine, if desired. Makes about 24.

Corn Bread (pictured on pages 54 and 55)

1 cup all-purpose flour
1 cup yellow cornmeal
¼ cup sugar
4 teaspoons baking powder
¾ teaspoon salt
2 eggs
1 cup milk
¼ cup cooking oil *or* shortening,
    melted

Stir together flour, cornmeal, sugar, baking powder, and salt. Add eggs, milk, and oil or melted shortening. Beat just till smooth (do not overbeat). Turn into greased 9x9x2-inch baking pan. Bake in 425° oven for 20 to 25 minutes. Makes 8 or 9 servings.

Corn Sticks: Prepare Corn Bread batter as above. Spoon batter into greased corn stick pans, filling pans ⅔ full. Bake in 425° oven for 12 to 15 minutes. Makes 20 sticks.

Confetti Corn Bread

1 14-ounce package corn bread
    mix
1 teaspoon minced dried onion
¼ teaspoon dried thyme, crushed
2 slightly beaten eggs
1 cup water
2 tablespoons chopped pimiento
2 tablespoons chopped canned
    green chili peppers

In mixing bowl stir together packaged corn bread mix, minced onion, and thyme. In small mixing bowl combine beaten eggs, water, chopped pimiento, and green chili peppers; add all at once to dry ingredients, stirring just till moistened. Turn batter into a well-greased 9x9x2-inch baking pan. Bake in 400° oven for 20 to 25 minutes or till golden. Cut into squares to serve. Makes 9 servings.

Southern Corn Bread

¼ cup bacon drippings
1 cup cornmeal
1 cup all-purpose flour
1 tablespoon baking powder
½ teaspoon baking soda
½ teaspoon salt
2 beaten eggs
1 cup buttermilk

Put bacon drippings in a 10-inch oven-going skillet. Heat in 425° oven till drippings are melted.

In large mixing bowl stir together cornmeal, flour, baking powder, baking soda, and salt. Combine eggs and buttermilk; add to cornmeal. Slowly pour the melted bacon drippings into the cornmeal-buttermilk mixture, stirring just till smooth. Turn batter into the *hot greased skillet*. Bake in 425° oven about 20 minutes or till golden. Serve warm with butter or margarine, if desired. Makes 6 servings.

Note: Baking in a hot greased skillet gives the corn bread crisp edges.

Spoon Bread

2 cups milk
1 cup yellow cornmeal
1 cup milk
2 tablespoons butter *or* margarine
1 teaspoon salt
1 teaspoon baking powder
3 beaten egg yolks
3 stiff-beaten egg whites
    Butter *or* margarine

In saucepan stir 2 cups milk into cornmeal. Cook, stirring constantly, till very thick and pulling away from sides of pan. Remove from heat. Stir in 1 cup milk, 2 tablespoons butter or margarine, salt, and baking powder. Stir about *1 cup* of the hot mixture into egg yolks; return to saucepan. Gently fold in egg whites. Turn into greased 2-quart casserole. Bake in 325° oven about 50 minutes or till knife inserted near center comes out clean. Serve immediately with butter or margarine. Makes 6 servings.

Cheese Spoon Bread: Prepare Spoon Bread batter as above, *except* stir ½ cup grated *parmesan cheese* (2 ounces) into cooked cornmeal mixture with the 2 tablespoons butter or margarine.

Pancakes, Waffles, and Popovers

Pancakes

1¼ **cups all-purpose flour**
2 **tablespoons granulated sugar**
2 **teaspoons baking powder**
½ **teaspoon salt**
1 **beaten egg**
1 **cup milk**
1 **tablespoon cooking oil**

In mixing bowl stir together flour, granulated sugar, baking powder, and salt. Combine egg, milk, and oil; add all at once to flour mixture, stirring till blended but still slightly lumpy (step 1). Pour about ¼ *cup* batter onto hot, lightly greased griddle or heavy skillet for each standard-size pancake *or* about *1 tablespoon* batter for each dollar-size pancake (step 2). Cook till golden brown, turning to cook other side when pancakes have a bubbly surface and slightly dry edges (step 3). Makes about eight 4-inch pancakes or about 30 dollar-size pancakes.

Buttermilk Pancakes: Prepare Pancake batter as above, *except* reduce baking powder to *1 teaspoon* and add ½ teaspoon *baking soda* to the flour mixture; substitute 1⅓ cups *buttermilk or sour milk* for the 1 cup milk. Add additional buttermilk to thin the batter, if necessary. Makes about 10 pancakes.

Buckwheat Pancakes: Prepare Pancake batter as above, *except* substitute ¾ cup *whole wheat flour* and ½ cup *buckwheat flour* for the 1¼ cups all-purpose flour and substitute 2 tablespoons *brown sugar* for the granulated sugar. Increase milk to *1¼ cups.* Makes about 8 pancakes.

Feather Pancakes: Prepare Pancake batter as above, *except* use 2 beaten *egg yolks* instead of 1 beaten egg; beat 2 *egg whites* till stiff peaks form and fold into the batter. Makes about 12 pancakes.

1

Add egg-milk-oil mixture all at once to flour mixture. Adding liquid ingredients all at once helps prevent overbeating.

Stir only till mixture is blended. Batter will be slightly lumpy, as shown. These lumps will disappear during baking.

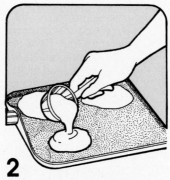

2

When griddle is hot, dip out about ¼ *cup* batter for each pancake, as shown. This amount of batter will make standard-size cakes. For dollar-size pancakes, use a tablespoonful of batter. Be sure to space the batter far enough apart so that the pancakes will not touch as they expand.

3

Pancakes are ready to turn when tops are bubbly all over, with a few broken bubbles, as shown. Edges of the pancakes will be slightly dry. Turn the pancakes only once. To turn, use a broad spatula.

Keep cooked pancakes warm by piling them on a paper-lined baking sheet in a warm oven. Put paper toweling between each layer to absorb the steam.

Orange-Bran Pancakes

¾ **cup all-purpose flour**
¼ **cup whole bran cereal**
2 **tablespoons wheat germ**
2 **teaspoons baking powder**
½ **teaspoon baking soda**
½ **teaspoon salt**
½ **teaspoon grated orange peel**
1 **beaten egg**
1 **cup orange juice**
2 **tablespoons cooking oil**
1 **cup maple-flavored syrup**
½ **teaspoon grated orange peel**

In large mixing bowl stir together the flour, bran cereal, wheat germ, baking powder, baking soda, salt, and ½ teaspoon grated orange peel.

In small mixing bowl beat together egg, orange juice, and cooking oil. Add egg mixture to flour mixture all at once. Stir till blended but still slightly lumpy.

Pour about ¼ *cup* batter for each pancake onto hot, lightly greased griddle or heavy skillet. Cook till golden brown, turning to cook other side when pancakes have a bubbly surface and slightly dry edges. Meanwhile, in small saucepan stir together maple-flavored syrup and ½ teaspoon orange peel; heat through. Serve over pancakes. Makes 8 pancakes.

Easy Potato Pancakes

½ **of a 12-ounce package (1 cup)**
frozen fried hash brown
potatoes
1 **cup packaged pancake mix**
¼ **cup finely chopped onion**
¼ **teaspoon salt**
Dash pepper
Maple-flavored syrup (optional)

Rinse and separate hash brown potatoes in hot water; drain well. In mixing bowl prepare pancake mix according to package directions. Stir in potatoes, chopped onion, salt, and pepper. Pour about ¼ *cup* batter for each pancake onto hot, lightly greased griddle or heavy skillet. Cook till golden brown, turning to cook other side when pancakes have a bubbly surface and slightly dry edges. Serve with maple-flavored syrup, if desired. Makes 12 to 14 pancakes.

Whole Wheat Pancakes

1¼ **cups whole wheat flour**
¾ **cup all-purpose flour**
2 **tablespoons brown sugar**
4 **teaspoons baking powder**
½ **teaspoon salt**
2 **beaten eggs**
2 **cups milk**
3 **tablespoons cooking oil *or***
shortening, melted
Honey Syrup

In bowl stir together whole wheat flour, all-purpose flour, brown sugar, baking powder, and salt. Beat together eggs, milk, and oil or melted shortening. Add all at once to dry ingredients, beating till blended but still slightly lumpy. Pour about ¼ *cup* batter for each pancake onto hot, lightly greased griddle or heavy skillet. Cook till golden brown, turning to cook other side when pancakes have a bubbly surface and slightly dry edges. Serve with Honey Syrup. Makes 16 pancakes.

Honey Syrup: Heat together ⅓ cup *honey* and ⅓ cup *maple-flavored syrup.*

Applesauce Pancakes

1½ **cups all-purpose flour**
2 **tablespoons sugar**
1 **tablespoon baking powder**
¼ **teaspoon salt**
⅛ **teaspoon ground nutmeg**
2 **beaten eggs**
1 **cup milk**
1 **cup applesauce**
2 **tablespoons butter *or***
margarine, melted

In large mixing bowl stir together flour, sugar, baking powder, salt, and nutmeg. In mixing bowl beat together eggs, milk, applesauce, and melted butter or margarine. Add egg mixture to flour mixture. Stir till blended but still slightly lumpy.

Pour about ¼ *cup* batter for each pancake onto hot, lightly greased griddle or heavy skillet. Cook till golden brown, turning to cook other side when pancakes have a bubbly surface and slightly dry edges. Serve with maple-flavored syrup, if desired. Makes about 14 pancakes.

French Toast

3 **beaten eggs**
¾ **cup milk**
1 **tablespoon sugar**
⅛ **teaspoon ground cinnamon**
   (optional)
10 **slices dry bread**
   Butter, margarine, *or* cooking oil
   Maple-flavored syrup *or*
      cinnamon-sugar

In shallow bowl beat together eggs, milk, sugar, cinnamon, and ¼ teaspoon *salt*. Dip bread in egg mixture, coating both sides. In skillet cook bread on both sides in a small amount of hot butter, margarine, or oil over medium-high heat till golden brown; add more butter as needed. Serve with maple-flavored syrup or cinnamon-sugar. Serves 5.

Orange French Toast

2 **beaten eggs**
½ **cup water**
3 **tablespoons frozen orange juice**
   concentrate
10 **slices day-old French bread, cut**
   ¾ **inch thick**
¾ **cup fine dry bread crumbs**
   Butter, margarine, *or* cooking oil
1 **cup light corn syrup**
2 **tablespoons frozen orange juice**
   concentrate

In shallow bowl beat together the eggs, water, and 3 tablespoons orange juice concentrate. Dip French bread slices into juice mixture, then into bread crumbs, coating evenly on both sides. In skillet cook French bread slices on both sides in a small amount of hot butter or oil over medium-high heat till golden; add more butter as needed.

Meanwhile, for orange syrup, in a small saucepan combine corn syrup and the 2 tablespoons orange juice concentrate. Bring to boiling; reduce heat and simmer 5 minutes. Pass hot syrup with toast. Makes 5 servings.

Coconut French Toast

2 **beaten eggs**
½ **cup milk**
1 **tablespoon sugar**
½ **cup chopped shredded coconut**
⅓ **cup crushed cornflakes**
6 **slices white bread**
   Butter, margarine, *or* cooking oil

In shallow dish beat together eggs, milk, and sugar. In another shallow dish combine coconut and cornflakes. Dip bread into egg mixture, then into coconut mixture, coating evenly on both sides. In skillet cook bread on both sides in a small amount of hot butter, margarine, or oil over medium-high heat till lightly browned, adding more butter as needed. Makes 3 servings.

Funnel Cakes

2 **beaten eggs**
1½ **cups milk**
2 **cups all-purpose flour**
1 **teaspoon baking powder**
½ **teaspoon salt**
2 **cups cooking oil**
   Powdered sugar
   Maple-flavored syrup (optional)

For batter, in mixing bowl combine beaten eggs and milk. Stir together flour, baking powder, and salt. Add to egg mixture; beat smooth with rotary beater.

In an 8-inch skillet heat cooking oil to 360°. Using a finger to cover the bottom opening of a funnel with a ½-inch spout (inside diameter), pour a generous ½ cup of batter into funnel. Remove finger and release batter into the hot oil, moving funnel in a circular motion to form a spiral. Cook about 2½ minutes or till golden brown. Using 2 wide metal spatulas, turn cake carefully. Cook about 1 minute more.

Drain on paper toweling; sprinkle with powdered sugar. Repeat with remaining batter. Serve warm cakes with maple-flavored syrup, if desired. Makes 4 or 5 cakes.

Waffles

1¾ cups all-purpose flour
1 tablespoon baking powder
½ teaspoon salt
2 egg yolks
1¾ cups milk
½ cup cooking oil *or* shortening, melted
2 egg whites

In large mixing bowl stir together flour, baking powder, and salt. In small mixing bowl beat egg yolks with fork. Beat in milk and cooking oil or melted shortening. Add to flour mixture all at once. Stir mixture till blended but still slightly lumpy (step 1).

In small mixer bowl beat egg whites till stiff peaks form (step 2). Gently fold beaten egg whites into flour-milk mixture, leaving a few fluffs of egg white. *Do not overmix.*

Carefully pour batter onto grids of preheated, lightly greased waffle baker (step 3). Close lid quickly; do not open during baking. Use a fork to help lift the baked waffle off grid.

To keep baked waffles hot for serving, place in single layer on wire rack placed atop a baking sheet in warm oven. Makes three 9-inch waffles.

Pecan Waffles: Prepare Waffle batter as above, *except* sprinkle about 2 tablespoons broken *pecans* atop *each* waffle before closing lid to bake.

Corn Waffles: Prepare Waffle batter as above, *except* reduce milk to *1¼ cups* and add 1 cup canned *cream-style corn* to egg-milk mixture.

Spiced Waffles: Prepare Waffle batter as above, *except* add ½ teaspoon *ground cardamom or cinnamon* to the flour mixture; mix well.

1
Add egg-milk-oil mixture all at once to flour mixture. Adding liquid ingredients all at once helps prevent overbeating. Stir only till mixture is blended. Batter will be slightly lumpy, as shown. These lumps will disappear during baking.

2
In small mixer bowl beat egg whites till stiff peaks form (tips stand straight), as shown. This will take about 1 to 1½ minutes at medium speed of an electric mixer.

The beaten egg whites help give the waffles their light and airy texture.

3
Pour batter onto grids of a preheated, lightly greased waffle baker, as shown. Check manufacturer's directions for the recommended amount of batter to use with your waffle baker. Close lid quickly; do not open during baking. Waffles are done when steam stops escaping from sides of baker or when the indicator light comes on.

Banana Waffles

2 **cups Homemade Biscuit Mix (see recipe, page 81)** *or* **packaged biscuit mix**
2 **tablespoons sugar**
2 **beaten egg yolks**
1⅓ **cups milk**
½ **cup mashed banana**
2 **tablespoons cooking oil**
2 **stiff-beaten egg whites**

In mixing bowl stir together Homemade Biscuit Mix or packaged biscuit mix and sugar. Combine egg yolks, milk, mashed banana, and cooking oil. Add to dry ingredients all at once, stirring till blended but still slightly lumpy.

Carefully fold in beaten egg whites, leaving a few fluffs of egg white in batter. *Do not overmix.* Pour batter onto grids of preheated, lightly greased waffle baker. Close lid quickly; do not open during baking. Carefully remove waffle from grid with a fork. Repeat with remaining batter. Makes three 9-inch waffles.

Buttermilk Waffles

1¾ **cups all-purpose flour**
2 **teaspoons baking powder**
½ **teaspoon baking soda**
½ **teaspoon salt**
2 **beaten egg yolks**
2 **cups buttermilk**
½ **cup cooking oil** *or* **shortening, melted**
2 **stiff-beaten egg whites**

In mixing bowl stir together flour, baking powder, baking soda, and salt. Combine egg yolks, buttermilk, and cooking oil or melted shortening. Add to flour mixture all at once. Stir mixture till blended but still slightly lumpy.

Carefully fold in beaten egg whites, leaving a few fluffs of egg white. *Do not overmix.*

Pour batter onto grids of preheated, lightly greased waffle baker. Close lid quickly; do not open during baking. Remove baked waffle from grid with a fork. Repeat with remaining batter. Makes four 9-inch waffles.

Chocolate Waffles

1 **beaten egg**
¾ **cup milk**
¼ **cup chocolate-flavored syrup**
2 **tablespoons cooking oil**
1 **cup packaged pancake mix**
⅓ **cup chopped pecans**

In mixer bowl beat together egg, milk, chocolate syrup, and cooking oil. Place pancake mix in large bowl. Add egg-chocolate mixture; beat just till blended.

Pour about *half* the batter onto grids of preheated, lightly greased waffle baker. Sprinkle with *half* of the nuts. Close lid quickly; do not open during baking. Remove baked waffle from grid with a fork. Repeat with remaining batter and nuts. Makes two 9-inch waffles.

Cheese-and-Bacon Waffles

2 **cups Homemade Biscuit Mix (see recipe, page 81)** *or* **packaged biscuit mix**
¼ **cup bacon bits**
1 **tablespoon dried parsley flakes**
1 **tablespoon dried snipped chives**
½ **teaspoon celery salt**
1 **beaten egg**
1⅓ **cups milk**
1 **teaspoon worcestershire sauce**
1 **cup shredded cheddar cheese**

In mixing bowl combine Homemade Biscuit Mix or packaged biscuit mix, bacon bits, parsley, chives, and celery salt. Beat together egg, milk, and worcestershire sauce. Add to dry ingredients all at once, stirring till blended but still slightly lumpy. Stir in cheese. Pour batter onto grids of preheated, lightly greased waffle baker. Close lid quickly; do not open during baking. Remove baked waffle from grid with a fork. Repeat with remaining batter. Makes three 9-inch waffles.

Popovers

1½ teaspoons shortening
2 beaten eggs
1 cup milk
1 tablespoon cooking oil
1 cup all-purpose flour
½ teaspoon salt

Grease six 6-ounce custard cups with ¼ *teaspoon* of the shortening for *each* cup. Place custard cups on a 15x10x1-inch baking pan or baking sheet and place in oven; preheat oven to 450°. Meanwhile, in 4-cup liquid measure or mixing bowl combine beaten eggs, milk, and oil. Add flour and salt (step 1). Beat with electric mixer or rotary beater till mixture is smooth (step 2). Remove pan from oven. Fill the hot custard cups *half* full. Return to oven (step 3). Bake in 450° oven for 20 minutes. Reduce oven to 350° and bake 15 to 20 minutes more or till popovers are *very* firm. (If popovers brown too quickly, turn off oven and finish baking in the cooling oven till very firm.) A few minutes before removing from oven, prick each popover with a fork to let steam escape. Serve hot. Makes 6 popovers.

Note: If you like popovers dry and crisp, turn off the oven after popovers are completely baked. Leave them in oven 30 minutes more with door ajar.

Blender Popovers: Prepare Popover batter as above, *except* combine eggs, milk, oil, flour, and salt in blender container. Cover and blend about 30 seconds or till combined. Scrape down sides as necessary.

Cinnamon Popovers: Prepare Popover batter as above, *except* add 1 teaspoon *ground cinnamon* to egg mixture.

Pecan Popovers: Prepare Popover batter as above, *except* stir ¼ cup finely chopped *pecans* into batter.

Whole Wheat Popovers: Prepare Popover batter as above, *except* use only ⅔ *cup* all-purpose flour and substitute ⅓ cup *whole wheat flour*.

1
Combine beaten eggs, milk, and oil in 4-cup liquid measure or mixing bowl. Add flour and salt (sifting is not necessary). Flour forms gluten when mixed with a liquid. As the batter is beaten, the gluten develops an elastic quality that later allows it to stretch, forming a shell around the expanding steam.

2
Using an electric mixer or rotary beater, beat for 1 to 1½ minutes or till smooth. (The popover batter will be thin.) Avoid excessive beating, which will result in popovers that have a rough, heavy texture.

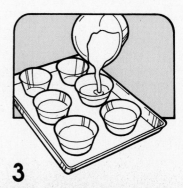

3
Remove hot greased custard cups on baking pan from preheated oven. Carefully pour batter from liquid measure or bowl into prepared cups, filling each cup about ½ full. Slide baking pan into preheated oven to bake. Do not open oven door during baking. Opening the oven door lets in cool air, which will condense the steam inside popovers and cause them to collapse.

Bread Fix-Ups

Choose a Bread

French or Italian Bread: Cut a *1-pound loaf* into 1-inch diagonal slices, cutting to, but not through, bottom crust. Spread your choice of filling mixture between every other slice of bread. Wrap loosely in foil. Place on baking sheet. Heat in 350° oven about 20 minutes or till hot throughout. Makes about 15 servings.

Dinner or Hard Rolls: Split 10 to 12 *dinner rolls* in half vertically. (For hard rolls, split each roll horizontally, cutting to, but not through, opposite side of roll.) Spread your choice of filling mixture on cut surfaces of each roll; reassemble rolls. Wrap loosely in foil. Place on baking sheet. Heat in 350° oven for 15 to 20 minutes or till hot throughout. Makes 10 to 12 servings.

Rye or Wheat Bread: Spread your choice of filling mixture on one side of 12 *bread slices.* Place slices together, forming 6 sandwiches; stack sandwiches. Wrap loosely in foil. Heat in 350° oven about 20 minutes or till hot throughout. Pull slices apart to serve. Makes 12 servings.

Pick a Spread

Mustard-Parsley Spread: Combine 6 tablespoons *butter or margarine,* softened; 2 tablespoons finely snipped *parsley;* 2 teaspoons prepared *mustard;* and ½ teaspoon dried *oregano,* crushed.

Garlic Spread: Stir together 6 tablespoons *butter or margarine,* softened; and ½ teaspoon *garlic powder.*

Parmesan Spread: Stir together 6 tablespoons *butter or margarine,* softened; ¼ cup grated *parmesan cheese;* and 1 tablespoon snipped *chives.*

Caraway-Cheese Spread: Stir together one 4-ounce container *whipped cream cheese with pimiento,* 1 tablespoon thinly sliced *green onion,* and 1 teaspoon *caraway seed.*

Cheesy Butter Spread: Cream together ¾ cup shredded *Swiss, cheddar, monterey jack, or American cheese;* ¼ cup *butter or margarine,* softened; 2 tablespoons finely snipped *parsley;* and 2 teaspoons prepared *horseradish.*

Herbed Spread: Cream together 6 tablespoons *butter or margarine,* softened; ½ teaspoon dried *marjoram,* crushed; ½ teaspoon dried *thyme,* crushed; and ¼ teaspoon *garlic powder.*

Index